GUIDE
3D
3D3D
TRIDIMENSIONAL
OF
Buenos Aires

GUIDE
3D 3D 3D
TRIDIMENSIONAL
OF
Buenos Aires

TRIDIMENSION

BUE

A

Edithor / Author:
Daniel Santoro

Luis Sáenz Peña 235 1º piso.
Tel and fax: 4371-7690

Staff:
Design: *Marcelo Rolla -*
Daniel Santoro.
Drawings: *Daniel Santoro.*
Maps: *ZGROUP s.a.*
Photography: *Otilio Moralejo and*
Daniel Santoro. Teatro Colón
Photography by Raquel Bigio.
Text: *Liliana Cascales -*
Daniel Santoro.
Translator: *Gabriela Gebl, Victoria*
Rodil, María Gloria Municoy and
Sandra Levy
Assistants: *Luciano, Francisco y*
Sofia Santoro.
Distribution: *María Pinto*
Thanks to: *Carlos Copelo and*
Alicia Monti, tango dancers, pho-
tography models.

ISBN: 987-05-0089-7

Preimpretion: **ZGROUP sa**
Uruguay 328 1º 1
Tel.: 4374-9229
e-mail: info@zgroupsa.com.ar

Edition Year 2006

L GUIDE OF
NOS
RES

Contents

Airlines

AEROCANCUN
- Tel: 4374-0909

AEROFLOT
- Av. Santa Fe 1558
  Piso 5°. Tel 4312-5573

AEROLINEAS ARGENTINAS
- Bouchard 547
  Tel 4340.-7777

aeroperu
- Av. Santa Fe 840
  Tel 4311-4115

AIR FRANCE
- Paraguay 610
  Tel 4317-4700

Alitalia
- Esmeralda 1111 28°
  Tel: 4310-9999

American Airlines
- Av. Santa Fe 881
  Tel 4318-1111

AUSTRAL
- Av. L.N. Alem 1134
  Tel 4317-3600

Avianca
- C. Pellegrini 1163
  Tel: 4322-2731

BRITISH AIRWAYS
- Córdoba 650
  Tel 4320-6600

Canadian
- Av. Córdoba 656
  Tel: 4322-3632

cubana
- Sarmiento 552
  Tel 4327-2244

DINAR
- C. Pellegrini 675
  Tel 4327-22244

ECUATORIANA
- Suipacha 1065
  Tel 4311-3010

IBERIA
- C. Pellegrini 1163
  Tel 4327-2739

KLM
- Tel 4312-2660

Southern Winds SW
- Florida 868 - 13° E
  Tel 4313-5883

LanChile
- Florida 954
  Tel. 4316-2200

Lufthansa
- M.T. de Alvear 636
  Tel: 4319-0600

LAB
- Tel 4326-5272

LAPA
- C. Pellegrini 1075
  Tel:4819-5272

malaysia
- Suipacha 1111 - 14°
  Tel 4313-4698

PLUNA
- Florida 1
  Tel 4342-4420

swissair
- Av. Santa Fe 846
  Tel: 4319-0000

UNITED AIRLINES
- Av. Madero 900
  Tel: 4316-07777

VARIG
- Pasaje Carabelas 344
  Tel 4329-9200

VASP
- Av. Santa Fe 784
  Tel 4312-8520

The legal currency in Argentina is called peso

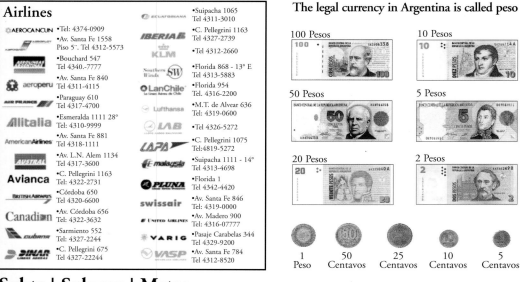

100 Pesos
10 Pesos
50 Pesos
5 Pesos
20 Pesos
2 Pesos

1 Peso | 50 Centavos | 25 Centavos | 10 Centavos | 5 Centavos

Subte | Subway | Metro

PREMETRO

COMPLEMENTARY NET OF BUSES

PARKINGS

BUSES

RAILWAYS

Public Holidays
January 1: New Year
May 1: Labor Day
May 25: May Revolution
June 20: Flag Day
July 9: Independence Day
August 17: Anniversary of General San Martin's death
October 12: Columbus Day
December 25: Christmas

Taxis
They are black and yellow in color and they are easily found on the city's main streets. You may hail a taxi on any corner but it is much safer to call one on the phone through radiotaxi services. The minimum fare is $ 1.60 and the passenger should pay the amount on the fare meter. A trip from Palermo to La Boca should not be more expensive than $ 6. Tipping is not required.

Bus (colectivo)
There are more than 150 bus lines in the city and the buses are easily seen on streets and avenues. The minimum fare for a trip within the city limits is $0.70 and the maximum fare is $ 0.80. Buses are furnished with automatic ticket machines that only accept coins.

Banks are open Monday through Friday from 10 AM to 3 PM. Shops are usually open from 9 AM to 8 PM. Shopping malls are open till 10 PM.

Tipping in restaurants and bars usually amounts to 10 % of the bill, though it will not be included in the bill.

Pay telephones may take either coins or calling cards, which may be found out by reading the message on the screen before using the phone.

Subway Lines
Five subway lines and one Pre-Metro line run across most tourist-attractive areas in the city and the service is quite good and inexpensive ($ 0.70 and 0.35). The fare is paid through tokens, which may be purchased in any station. The following are the names and areas covered by each line:
Line A: It runs under Av de Mayo and Av. Rivadavia. It goes from Plaza de Mayo to Primera Junta and it has a stop at Congress Square.
Line B: It runs under Av. Corrientes. It goes from Leandro N. Alem station (behind the Argentina Postal Service Building) to Chacarita station. It stops at the Abasto market (Carlos Gardel station).
Line C: It runs under Av. 9 de Julio and other streets. It goes from Constitución station to Retiro station. You may change in Diagonal Norte station for the rest of the lines. It has a stop at San Martín Square.
Line D: It goes from the Cathedral in Plaza de Mayo to José Hernández station in Barrancas de Belgrano quarter. On its way to Barrio Norte, it stops at Callao station, Agüero station, Facultad de Medicina station (under the Medicine College of the University of Buenos Aires) and Palermo station. After that, it runs under Cabildo Avenue.
Line E: It runs under Av. San Juan and it goes form Plaza de Mayo to Virreyes station, where you may change for the Pre-Metro line.
Pre-Metro: It goes form Virreyes station to a theme park called Parque de la Ciudad. The fare is $ 0.25 for those who take it on Virreyes station, but it is free for those who are changing from Line E.

Brief history of the city of Buenos Aires

First foundation

When facing the need to stop the Portuguese forces' advance, Carlos I, king of Spain, sent commander Pedro de Mendoza to establish a stone fort somewhere in the Río de la Plata area. This fort would serve as the origin for a new city.

In 1536, Pedro de Mendoza arrived in the Rio de la Plata banks with around 2,000 men and he found the right place to establish his fort on a high hill by the rivulet's outlet. He had some thatch-roofed mud huts built on a compact earth slope where we can find Lezama Park today. In the beginning, good relationships with Native Americans allowed him to exchange low-value articles for food and other necessities. However, it was not long before this harmony came to an end and famine struck, which caused the population not only to decrease seriously due to confrontations but also to witness awful cannibalism scenes.

Image of Buenos Aires in 1536 (First Foundation).

Second foundation

In 1580, a new expedition departed from Paraguay. This time it was Juan de Garay who founded the base for the second time. He gave this settlement the name of "Ciudad de la Santísima Trinidad y Puerto de Santa María de los Buenos Ayres". The site he chose was two kilometers north of the first settlement and there he planted the tree of justice as a symbol for the generations to come.

This is a picture by Santiago Carbonell where we can see the scene of the foundation of Buenos Aires in front of the tree of justice, where Plaza de Mayo stands today.

As ordered under the Laws of the Indies, town planners used a checkerboard plan for the layout of the town. The plan featured a Plaza Mayor or central square, 15 blocks from North to South and 9 blocks from East to West. The only opening in the checkerboard was the Plaza Mayor (currently Plaza de Mayo), where enough space was left for a fortress. The city underwent the first change in 1594 when a stone wall was built for the fortress, which was only finished in 1713.

In the 17th Century, the city's population was 27,000 people. Increase in commercial activity together with smuggling and slaves commerce allowed the city to start expanding rapidly.

Tridimensional Guide of Buenos Aires

British Invasions:

In 1800, the British Empire started implementing its colonialist expansion policies. The second step in their plan, after winning the battle in Cabo de la Buena Esperanza, was undertaking the Rio de la Plata area. In 1806, an English commander called Beresford disembarked with his troops in the south of the city. The first British invasion lasted 46 days and Liniers, from Montevideo, planned the recovery of the area. In 1807, another invasion took place and was repelled thanks to a heroic defense carried out by the local population, who later created the first body of Argentinian soldiers, called Patricios.

British troops surrendering to Santiago de Liniers in 1806.

Independence:

In 1810, after the Napoleonic War in Spain, a group of prominent citizens decided to request that the viceroy be dethroned and replaced by an autonomous governing body, the form of which was not still clear.

On July 9, 1816, delegates from both the Capital City and the rest of the country proclaimed absolute independence from the king of Spain.

Once Independence was proclaimed, a fratricidal struggle took place between the city of Buenos Aires and the rest of the provinces in order to determine the system of goernment for the new nation. In 1850, started growing steadily due to the new political organization in the country. New quarters called Constitución, La Boca and Retiro joined the urban checkerboard. To the west, the city expanded towards a town called Flores and, by 1880, the population had reached 300,000 inhabitants. Health and environmental conditions were not improved as the city grew. Between 1867 and 1871, 20,000 people died of cholera and yellow fever because there was no water system whatsoever and garbage was thrown into the many creeks that ran across the city. When the cholera and yellow fever plagues hit Buenos Aires, the wealthiest families, who lived in the southern areas, were forced to move north.

Inmigration:

In 1880, during President Roca's administration, the Federal Capital district of the Argentine Republic was established in the city of Buenos Aires. Torcuato de Alvear, mayor of the city in those times, decided that Buenos Aires should become the Paris of South America. He then had the Old Market (Vieja Recova) demolished, opened Av. De Mayo and developed a new urban area around Av Alvear and Barrio Norte. By 1914, and thanks to emigrants, the city's population had grown eight-fold. The first signals of modern times started to appear in 1920, when the first skyscraper (Barolo building) was built and the first subway lines began working, but it was only in the 1950s that urban development made Buenos Aires one of the biggest cities in the world. During the subsequent decades, the city took its current shape due to the growth of high-rise buildings. In the 1970s, a highway network converging in the city's center was incorporated into Buenos Aires. The error in selection of the converging point caused serious traffic problems, which are accountable for high pollution rates in the downtown area.

Nowadays, the city's population is 3 million inhabitants and the number of people living in the suburban area exceeds 9 million.

View of Plaza de Mayo in the middle-18th Century. The main building is the fortress that stood where the Executive Office Building stands today.

Avenida de Mayo in the early 20th Century.

View of the port in front of the Customs Building,

Map of the city with suggested tours

Reserva Ecológica

15•

16•

18•

OLAYA
HIDALGO
ACOYTE
CAMPICHUELO
OTAMENDI
RIO DE JANEIRO
17•

PARQUE CENTENARIO

L. MARECHAL
PADILLA
CAMARGO

AV. 25 DE MAYO

AV. ENTRE RIOS

14•
Plaza de los dos Congresos

12•

13•

AV. RIVADAVIA

AV. DE MAYO

AV. CORRIENTES

Obelisco

AV. 9 DE JULIO

AV. MONTES DE OCA

3•

Plaza Dorrego

AV. SAN JUAN

AV. INDEPENDENCIA

AV. BELGRANO

1•
Plaza de Mayo

AV. DE MAYO

AV. CORRIENTES

Parque LEZAMA

AV. REG. PATRICIOS

AV. PASEO COLON

2•

AV. L. N. LEM

AV. LUIS HUERGO

AV. E. MADERO

4•
AV. ALTE. BROWN

Casa Amarilla

AV. ALICIA MOREAU DE JUSTO

DIQUE 1

DIQUE 2

DIQUE 3

DIQUE 4

BVRD. FH. PENDOZA

BVRD. A. VILLAFLOR

BVRD. M. GUEMES

AV. ALMIRANTE BROWN

AV. BRASIL

5•

BVRD. DE LOS ITALIANOS

AV. INT. MARTIN NOEL

9 Pza. Italia

AV. SARMIENTO

Jardín Botanico   Jardín Zoologico

Rosedal

AV. CORONEL DIAZ

AV. LAS HERAS

AV. DEL LIBERTADOR

AV. FIGUEROA ALCORTA

Bosques de Palermo

Aeroparque
Jorge Newbery

AV. CORDOBA

11

Pza. Houssay

AV. CORDOBA

AV. CALLAO

Pza. Rodriguez Peña

8

AV. LAS HERAS

AV. PUEYRREDON

Pza. Chile

10

Pza. Mitre

AV. FIGUEROA ALCORTA

Recoleta   Pza. Francia

Pza. Vicente Lopez

AV. CALLAO

AV. ALVEAR

AV. ARTURO ILLIA

Pza. Carlos Pellegrini

7

AV. 9 DE JULIO

AV. SANTA FE

6

AV. DEL LIBERTADOR

AV. CORDOBA

Plaza San Martin

Retiro

Puerto Nuevo

RIO DE LA PLATA

The purpose of this travel guide is to show you the most interesting parts of the city through a visual ride. Although Buenos Aires is an enormous city, the 14 tours we suggest comprise each and every point of interest for those travelers who will spend just a few days in the Capital of Tango.

"The first impression when arriving in Buenos Aires is that of finding the last part of the world which can hold a big city.
In its condition as the last city on Earth, it ends up comprising any other city in the world and reminding us of them.
The second impression is that of the endless. An endlessly big geographical area which is reflected in what is endlessly urban about Buenos Aires..."

Franco Purini

Tour from Buenos Aires

Plaza de Mayo and surrounding area

Eva Perón and Juan Domingo Perón.

Mothers of Plaza de Mayo.

Plaza de Mayo is the original center of the city's historic area, which was founded by Juan de Garay in 1580.

Ever since 1810 it has been the scene of every major political event in the country. In 1880, Juan Buschiazzo carried out an important remodeling of the square in search of the classical symmetry that can still be recognized there. Some years later, French landscape designer Charles Thays gave the square its current looks. Its surrounding area grew when Av. de Mayo was opened, together with Diagonal Norte and Diagonal Sur streets, and when the City, as we call our downtown area, was developed.

Both in the square and it surrounding area, we can find architectural samples from different periods: the Cabildo, the Pyramid of May and the Cathedral date from the colonial period (18th Century and early 19th Century).

The Executive Office Building (Casa Rosada or Pink House) and the Municipal Building (former Hotel Victoria) date from the late-19th Century /early-20th Century period.

The Ministry of Economy (former Mortgage Bank) and the National Bank buildings belong to the monumental style developed by the government during the 1930s and the 1940s. Plaza de Mayo was the place where Evita was acclaimed as a political figure and were the Peronist Party was born. In 1976, during the last coup in Argentina, the square became internationally known due to the presence of the Mothers of Plaza de Mayo, who would walk around the Pyramid every Thursday claiming for their "disappeared" sons and daughters.

In 1983, the square also witnessed the restoration of democracy. We suggest sitting on one of the benches protected by trees to watch the intense activity in the City and enjoy the views, both of the Obelisk at the end of Diagonal Norte street and of the many belfries and domes along Av. De Mayo.

Plaza de Mayo and surrounding area in 3d

Equestrian Statue of General Roca: *He directed the conquest of the Patagonic desert, therefore integrating the whole territory of Argentina and exterminating many Native American tribes.*

Manzana de Las Luces. or Block of Light (see p. 23).

Pirámide de Mayo (see p. 18).

City's Museum (see p. 26).

Ethnography Museum. Juan B. Ambrosetti. Moreno 350 (see p.26).

San Francisco's Convent and Church: *Construction of the Convent started in 1587 and the Church's original building dates from 1754. In the church you may find a beautiful piece of tapestry by visual artist Horacio Butler. The current front of the building was designed in an eclectic style during the late 19th Century. The enormous dome is awesome and it can be seen from the corner of Moreno and Defensa streets. If you take a walk around the block, you will find a group of houses built during the same period. (see p. 18)*

City's Legislature Building (see p. 21).

Diagonal Julio A. Roca

Chacabuco

Perú

Bolivar

Moreno

Defensa

Adolfo Alsina

Hipolito Yrigoyen

Balcarce

Former Banco Hipotecario or Mortgage Bank.

Paseo Colón

Equestrian Statue of General Belgrano: *It was formally unveiled in 1873 and it was created by French sculptor Albert.*

Museum of History of the Executive Office Building. *Hipolito Yrigoyen 219.* **Horario:** *Monday to Friday, 10:00 to 18:00. Free.*

Cabildo *(see p. 18).*

Culture's house ex edificio la prensa.

City's Executive Office Building.

Av. de Mayo

Maipú

Rivadavia

Perú

Diagonal R. Sáenz Peña

Calle Florida

AV. DE MAYO

San Martín

Reconquista

Bme. Mitre

25 de Mayo

Leandro N. Alem

Corner of Diagonal Norte and Florida streets: *You may find huge domes and an interesting neocolonial building owned by the Bank of Boston with a shocking entrance door and hall in Plateresque style. If you walk down Florida street, you will get to San Martín Square and Retiro.*

Catedral Metropolitana: *(see p.19).*

National Bank of Argentina.

Executive Office Building (Casa Rosada or Pink House): *It is built on the site chosen by Garay for the city's fortress in 1580. The building has undergone many changes. In 1882, two twin buildings were the seat of the Executive Office and they were later joined by means of an archway which is now the main entrance, looking on Plaza de Mayo. In 1873, President Sarmiento had it painted pink and it remained so until now.*

Monument to Cristobal Colón.

The Cabildo

It was originally the seat of the city's government and its construction finished in 1764. At the back of the Cabildo there is a big patio where the jail for male prisoners used to be. When Av. De Mayo was opened, in 1889, a third of the original building was demolished and the same thing happened again when Diagonal Sur street was created.

The cabildo was of great importance during the events that led to the proclamation of independence from Spanish rule in 1810.

Its current appearance should be thanked to a detailed restoration work undertaken in 1939. In the patio behind the building, you will find a walkway that joins Hipólito Yrigoyen street with Av de Mayo. This is the ideal place to take a break and breathe the air of colonial Buenos Aires.

Inside the Cabildo there is a small crafts fair and an inexpensive fast-food restaurant.

Pyramid of May:
It was erected in 1811 to commemorate the events of May 1810. The original structure is still inside the current pyramid. It was created by Francisco Cañete.

Colonial yard

Ancient jail for men

Calle Hipólito Yrigoyen

Av. de Mayo

Entrance to Museum.

Walkway to Av. de Mayo.

Museum's ticket office.

Visiting Times:
Tuesday through Friday: 12:30 to 7 PM.
Sundays: 3 PM to 7 PM.
Guided tours on Sundays at 4 PM.

Executive Office Building (Casa Rosada or Pink House).

It has been erected where the Royal Fortress of San Juan Baltasar de Austria, which was built in 1595, used to stand. The Fortress has been restored many times and partly demolished for the construction of the New Custom House. During President Samiento's government, the building was painted pink, thus establishing a tradition still in use and giving the building its popular name.

President Roca asked architect Enrique Aberg to build a new Executive Office Building. In 1894, the Italian architect Francisco Tamburini planned a new building, creating the complex monument that can be seen today. The result is an eclectic building, where elements of diverse origin, such as the French mansards and the loggias and windows by Nordic architects, coexist in Tamburini's characteristic classic language.

Hall of Bust

Monumental Stairs.

White hall

Balcarce street

The Catedral

The original building dates from 1745 and the facade was modified in 1821 when a neoclassical gate was introduced according to the French trends of the time.

It was designated as Cathedral in 1836, once Joseph Dubourdieu had finished the magnificent new facade, which represents Jacob with his son, Joseph. (You may see it from the square across the street).

If you enter the building and walk along the nave to your right, when you get to the fourth column you will find a chapel containing the mausoleum of General San Martín. Soldiers of the Granaderos corps, a branch of the army created by General San Martín himself, permanently guard the site.

Next to the first column on the right nave you may see a Russian icon, Our Lady of Vladimir, and also an image of Our Lady of the Forsaken, which was created in Sevilla during the 18th Century. Both the alta piece on the main altar and the paintings in it date from the late 18th Century period.

The Monumental Colonnade: *It faces Rivadavia street and it reminds us of the Madelaine Church or the Bourbon Palace in Paris.*

Cathedral (inside view): *The inside of the Cathedral was designed in a sober baroque style. In the picture you may see the rich ornaments in the altar, which was recently restored together with all the lateral chapels.*

> **Guided tours:** *Monday through Friday at 1 PM. Saturdays at 11:30 AM. Sundays at 10 A.M.*
> *Meeting point: entrance to the nave on your right.*

Icon of Our Lady of the Forsaken, late 18th Century.

Mausoleum of General San Martín.

Meeting point for guided tours.

General San Martín: *He is the most important Argentinian hero. Liberator of the American continent, he is called "Father of the Nation".*

These twelve columns represent the twelve Apostles.

Main altarpiece, 18th Century.

Altarpiece of the Main Altar: *Icon of the Immaculate Virgin. 18th Century.*

Avenida de Mayo Between Perú Street and Plaza de Mayo

Former building of "La Prensa" (newspaper) and current House of Culture.

In 1910, after a visit to Buenos Aires, George Clemenceau said: "Undoubtedly, the most sumptuous building is that of the opulent La Prensa, which is known to be the main newspaper in South America".

In a prominently French style, you may see superb pieces of blacksmithing on gates and lamps. The inside of the entrance hall has recently been restored and it has recovered its famous original decoration, which is well worth a visit, as well as the Golden Hall on the first floor, where concerts and other cultural events are usually held.

Pasaje Roverano connection with Perú Subway Station.

Perú

Av. de Mayo

Perú Station Subway Line "A"

Portal de "La Prensa"

Perú Subway Station and Pasaje Roverano

On the same side of the street as the building of La Prensa you will find a subway station that belonged to the first subway line in Latin America. This station has been restored to its original condition by the City's Museum. A visit to Perú station will carry you to the Buenos Aires of the 1910s. If you walk across Av de Mayo from La Prensa building, you will see an interesting passage called Pasaje Roverano, which is connected with the subway station. You may find the connection by entering the passage's ground floor (see picture).

Building on the corner of Perú Street and Av. de Mayo.

Cortázar and the winners

On the corner of Perú street and Av de Mayo there stands a Liberty-style building that conveys a London-like atmosphere. The name of the cafeteria in the building is precisely London and it is an old and traditional shop, which has unfortunately been modernized. Part of the action in Julio Cortázar's novel "The Winners" develops in this cafeteria. Across Perú street, you may see a real display of luxurious buildings in a wide variety of Italian, French and Victorian styles. We suggest that you take a walk along Pasaje Urquiza Anchorena (on the odd-numbered sidewalk at 600). This passage joins Av de Mayo and Rivadavia street.

Julío Cortázar, Argentinian Writer

Rivadavia

Av. de Mayo

La Prensa Building. In this case, the sheltered central patio and the Golden Hall on the first floor facing Rivadavia street.

Legislature building of the City of Buenos Aires

This building was erected in 1930 by Architect Héctor Ayerza. It covers a big plot between Diagonal Sur street and Perú street and it is a sample of the eclectic trends in architecture during the firstdecades of this century. Its imposing neoclassical facade stretches along Diagonal Sur street and Perú street.

It has a very big and cozy library and there are also some halls designed for exhibitions on the ground floor. Halls San Martín and El Dorado, which have been recently restored, deserve a visit.

The tower is almost 90 meters high and on top of it there is a unique carillon for a clock that is still at work.

90 meters tower with carillon

Representatives Chamber

Entrance to Library

Perú

Entrance to exhibition halls

Main entrance to halls

Diagonal Julio A. Roca

Photo: Otilio Moralejo

Executive Office Building for the City of Buenos Aires

Main entrance

Av. de Mayo

Bolivar

It was built between 1891 and 1902 by engeneer Juan María Cagnoni based on the original proyect by architect Juan Antonio Buschiazzo. The building was enlarged between 1912 and 1914 without considering said proyect.

The main entrance to the building is in Bolivar street 1. You walk up a white marble-stair covered by a red carpet.

At the entrance door, you will find the Flag Hall, where the guards watch the flag that the Executive Chief of the City of Buenos Aires hoists in Plaza de Mayo during national holidays.

The plot where the Executive Office Building is located is considered a historic place.

San Francisco church and monastery.
San Roque Parish

On Alsina and Defensa Streets.
It was built in 1730 by Jesuit architect Bianchi. Its final reconstruction was made by Arq. Sackmann in a German Barroc style. Some statues of San Francisco de Asís, Giotto, Dante Alighieri and Cristóbal Colón are placed on its facade. In the inner part, people can see a XX century tapestry made by argentine artist Horacio Buttler, containing a Virgin image, Franciscans tree, and San Francisco surrounded by animals and mendicants. San Roque Parish is one of the oldest churches in the city and it has a very important and valuable library.

San Francisco small square

It was built to give shelter to the great quantity of people who remained after religious ceremonies at San Francisco Church. The four statues which were located surrounding May Pyramid, have been replaced here at 1972 and they represent the Geography, Sailing, Astronomy and Industry.

Chapel of the Holy.

Elliptical dome.

San Roque's Church.

Tapiz de (8 x 12 meters), work of the painter Horacio Butler.

Defensa

Alsina

San Francisco's small square.

Archways, patio and vault of Procuraduría de las Misiones.

Neoclassical facade, 19th Century. Entrance to the cloisters of the Procuratie of the Missions (Procuraduría de las Misiones).

Facade of San Ignacio's Church: It was built in 1675. Inside the church you may find many altarpieces and pieces of imagery that date from the colonial period. Pay special attention to the rose stained-glass window at the back of the church.

Manzana de la Luces (Block of light)

The block is limited by the following streets: Perú, Alsina, Bolívar and Moreno. In 1616, this land was given to the Jesuits, who built San Ignacio's School and Church there. The church is currently at the corner of Bolívar and Alsina streets. The School of the Society of Jesus was demoished and the National

Calle Moreno

Former Representatives Chamber

Calle Perú

Guided Tours: *Fridays at 3 PM (free). Saturdays at 3 PM and 4:30 PM. Sundays at 3 PM, 4 PM and 5 PM. Meeting point: Perú 272.*

Courtyard of the Procuraduria

Diagonal South

Handicrafts marker

National Sachool of Buenos Aires.

Bolívar St.

Alsina St.

School of Buenos Aires was derected on the site, where it still stands today as the most traditional and prestigious school in the city.

The cloisters of the Procuraduría de las Misiones, which date from the late-17th Century period (the oldest in the city), stand on Perú street as well as the houses in numbers 222, 274 and 294.

The Jesuits were evicted in 1767 and the land was used for different purposes, such as location for the National School and University. These were the places were most of the intellectuals and literati that took part in the events leading to Argentinian Independence were educated. That is the reason why, in 1821, the area was called Manzana de las Luces (Block of Light) as a way to honor the men and women of letters who were educated there. We suggest that you start your visit at San Ignacio's Church, which was put up on the corner of Bolívar and Alsina streets in 1675. After that, you may visit the National School of Buenos Aires. It was built in 1911 and its monumental size is typically inspired by classical architecture. When you turn right at the corner of

San Ignacio Church

Map of the tunnels in the 18th Century, 6 meters underground

Bolívar and Moreno streets, you will find a colonial facade that belongs to the above mentioned houses. When you get to Perú street, you may wish to turn right and enter number 277, which has recently been restored and holds the former Representatives Chamber. If you keep on walking along Perú street, you will find, in number 222, the oldest building in the block, which used to belong to the Procuraduría de las Misiones. As you

approach the corner of Perú street and Diagonal Sur, you may find the entrance to a handicrafts market. Another interesting spot you might wish to visit in the Block of Light is that of the tunnels which run under it. They were built around 6 meters deep by the Jesuits in the 18th Century and they used to connect Jesuit temples with strategic places in the city.

Av. de Mayo and its interesting spots

Along Av de Mayo you will find many stores that sell used books, you may purchase interesting pieces at a low price.

Pedemonti Restaurant in Av de Mayo 676, traditional quality food, quite expensive.

Café Tortoni

San Miguel Palace

Av. 9 de Julio

B. de Hirigoyen

San Miguel Palace

C. Pellegrini

Tacuari

Piedras

Legislatura of the city of Buenos Aires

Chacabuco

Hipólito Yrigoyen

Suipacha

Pasaage Roverano

Cabildo

City hotel

Julio A. Roca

Perú

Av. de Mayo

Esmeralda

Bolívar

San Miguel Chuch

Pink House

Maipú

Defensa

Roberto Arlt square

Balcarce

Hipoólito Yrigoyen

Roque Saenz Peña

Florida

Pasaage Urquiza Anchorena

Av. Paseo Colón

Rivadavia

San Martín

London Bar

Reconquista

Former La Prensa Building, current House of Culture.

Av. Alem

Executive Office Building for the City of Buenos Aires.

De Mayo Square.

Tortoni Café, inside. It is always buzzing with activity and it has a Parisian atmosphere.

Front of Tortoni Café.

Tortoni Coffee

Av. de Mayo

Bust of Juan de Dios Filiberto by Luis Perlotti.

National Academy of Tango.

Cultural Vault, basement.

Bust of Benito Quinquela Martín

Bust of Borges

Bust of Julián Centeya, by Antonio Pujía.

Poets' Corner.

Tourist Information Office.

Shows hall.

Rivadavia St.

Alfonsina **STORNI**

Federico García **LORCA**

Jorge Luis **BORGES**

Our traditional Tortoni Café is located at the odd side of the street on Av de Mayo between Tacuarí and Piedras streets. It was one of the first cafés in the city and it used to be the meeting point for intellectuals and politicians. Nowadays, it serves as a real cultural center where jazz and tango events are usually held. If you take a leisurely walk inside the café and pay attention to the walls, you may find several commemorative objects for famous personalities of the arts, which have been placed in the spots where those people used to sit. Thus, you will see them over the tables at which Jorge Luis Borges, painter Quinquela Martín, poet and journalist Roberto Arlt, Federico García Lorca, poet Alfonsina Storni and others used to sit.

In the basement of an adjoining building we find what we call La Bodega or The Vault, a kind of café where shows are staged and where you will have the opportunity to listen to some excellent tango music. The National Academy of Tango, the muse of which is poet Horacio Ferrer, is on the ground floor of the same building. You may enter through the door next to Tortoni Café. At the back of the café, there is a small library called El Rincón de los Poetas, or Poets' Corner, where the city government has installed a tourist information office.

The café has two entrance doors: one of the faces Av de Mayo and the other one, Rivadavia street. If you go out through the second door, you will find Roberto Arlt Square across the street. This is another oasis where you will be able to forget the buzzing of the city for a moment. Behind the palos borrachos and other species of indigenous vegetation, you will have the opportunity to admire a huge mural in relief by visual artist Alberto Cedrón. The apse you will see from the square belongs to San Miguel Arcángel Church.

City's Museum

On the corner of Defensa and Alsina streets (Alsina 412) there stands the City's Museum. The building is a good sample of how a bourgeois house looked like by the end of the 19th Century. The Museum serves an important purpose, since it keeps the urban memories of the city alive through several restoration and preservation activities (see Perú subway station). On the first floor, the Museum usually exhibits interesting pieces of its collection depicting uses and customs of the city's population. On the ground floor, a drugstore called La Estrella (The Star) has been preserved in its original condition, as it looked when it was the Old Pharmacy of the area. On the same sidewalk of Alsina street, next door to the Museum, you will find Puerto Rico cafeteria, a perfect spot to take a break.

Articles rescued from demolition sites by the Museum.

Numerosos objetos de uso cotidiano se exhiben en el Museo pudiéndose ver siempre muestras originales, incluso restos de alguna demolición son puestos en valor por el Museo.

Household appliances from the Museum's collection. Inside view of the Museum.

City's Museum on the corner of Alsina and Defensa streets.

Opening time: Monday through Friday: 11 AM to 7 PM. Sundays: 3 PM to 7 PM. Special thanks to Eduardo Vazquez.

Etnographic museum Juan B. Ambrosetti

Moreno 350

Opening time.
Monday through Friday: 10 AM to 19 PM. Free Library consultant.
Tel.: 4331-7788

Library.

Offices and shops.

Expositions rooms

Moreno St.

On 350 Moreno St. It was created by Philosophy and Letters School in 1904. It has a valuable archeological collection from Argentine Patagonia and NorthWest, and from Africa and Oceanía.
The building was built at 1876 by Arq. Pedro Benoit to Law School of Buenos Aires University. The museum is located here from 1928.

Monserrat, Catedral al Sur

In the area bound by Plaza de Mayo and San Telmo quarter there are many places of interest as well as some streets and passages that stand out due to their shape.

The block called Santo Domingo was the area where a crucial battle took place during the British Invasion (see p. 28).

(see p. 28)

If you walk along Balcarce street and cross Belgrano Avenue until you arrive at Independencia street, you will pass by some of the best places where you can enjoy tango shows, dance and have dinner. They all open in the evening. We suggest that you have a drink and relax in some of the bars at the corner of Chile and Balcarce streets, it will allow you to penetrate the quiet atmosphere of the city's southern neighborhoods.

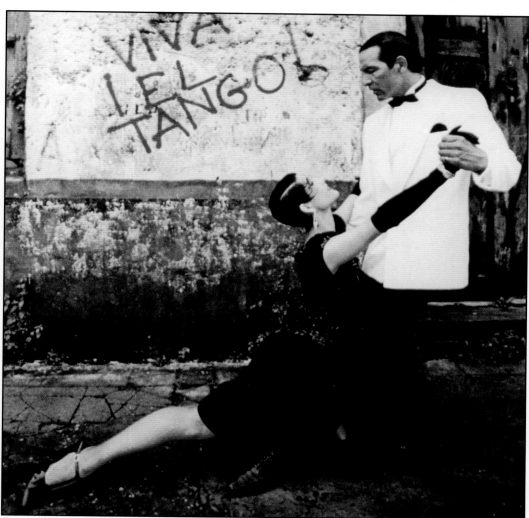

Dancers Alicia Monti and Carlos Copello

Catedral al Sur en 3 dimensiones

Sample of fantastic architecture with esoteric symbols, near the corner of Bolívar and Chile streets.

Detail of the entrance gate to José Hernandez's house.

Former National Library and current National Hall of Music: In this enormous neoclassical building, Borges worked as the director of the National Library for many years.

El zanjón de Granados.

Typical house with balconies on the corner of Defensa and San Lorenzo streets. This area is crowded with artists' studios, this making up the Argentinian Montmartre.

When you walk along San Lorenzo passage, you will find a narrow house that is called the "tiny house". It is only 2.30 meters wide.

Perú

Estados Unidos

Av. Independencia

Bolívar

Defensa

Psje. San Lorenzo

Chile

México

Balcarce

Av. Paseo Colón

San Lorenzo's Passage : Principled house of the 19th century.

The corner of Chile and Balcarce streets is the perfect spot to take a break. On the background, you may see the building of Antorchas, a foundation that promotes the arts.

Martin Fierro: José Hernández (1834-1886), an Argentinian poet and journalist born in Buenos Aires, is the author of *Martín Fierro*, a folk epic poem that is considered a national classic in Argentina.

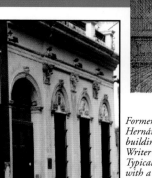

Former house of José Hernández and current building of the Argentine Writer's Association. Typical one-story house with a row of patios. It houses an important library and serves as location for several cultural activities.

Santo Domingo Church (see p. 30).

Piece of work by Alfredo Benavídez Bedoya, Argentinian engraver.

Museum of Engraving: a large old house at Defensa 372 serves as seat for the Museum of Engraving. It has collections of Argentinian engravers from the 19th and 20th Century on display. The institution carries out an intense activity and it regularly organizes exhibitions.

Opening time:
Monday through Saturday: 2 PM to 6 PM.
Sundays: 12 to 6 PM.
Guided tours: Sundays at 3 PM.

We suggest that you walk by number 350 Defensa street, next to the Museum of Engraving. There stands the house of Bernardino Rivadavia, the first president of Argentina, in its original condition (18th Century).

General Belgrano, designer of the Argentinian flag. His tomb is in the atrium of Santo Domingo Church.

Balcarce Street: Tango

Michelangelo,
Restaurant, Tangos.

Molière,
Cooffe, Restaurant, Bar, Tangos.

Taconeando, *Tango.*

La ventana,
*Restaurant,
Tango, Show.*

La Trastienda,
Espectáculos.

Casa Blanca,
Dinner, Tango, Show.

Our lady of Rosario Basilic
Santo Domingo Convent

Belgrano Av. and Defensa st. Its construction began in 1751 under the direction of Architect Antonio Masella. One of the towers was inaugurated at the end of XVIII century and the other one at the middle of last century. It keeps English flags, taken during English Invasions when they occupied the church and the flags from the royalists that Belgrano donated to the Virgin. Mausoleum of Gral Belgrano is located from the beginning of this century, in the atrium of the church. This is a work of Italian sculptor Ettore Ximenes. On the left tower, people can see replicas of the shots in 1807, because it has been reconstructed.

Monumental staircase called De Los Ingleses.

Cannon bullets, fingerprints of the English Invasions.

Universidad del Norte, Santo Tomás de Aquino

Organ.

Av. Belgrano

Defensa

Mausoleum of Manuel Belgrano designer of the Argentine flag.

Dressing-room of the Virgin. Chapel where are kept trophies of the reconquest of the city of Buenos Aires in 1807.

San Telmo Quarter

Our tour along the southern area of Buenos Aires continues along Defensa street until we get to Independencia Avenue, where we enter the San Telmo quarter. This quarter was born in 1735 as a hamlet in the outskirts of the city. Where Dorrego Square stands today, there used to be a residence for the Bethlehemite monks, south of the Lezama ranch (today, Museum of History and park).

The quarter's population was made up of aristocratic families until 1870, when they moved to the northern area of the city escaping the plagues partly caused by the poor health conditions in Buenos Aires. San Telmo then became a residential neighborhood and, in time, the large houses started to serve as tenement houses or conventillos where immigrants used to rent rooms, which led to growing deterioration of the buildings during the first half of the 20th Century.

It was only in the 1970s that some rules were established in order to preserve the quarter's buildings, thus keeping valuable pieces of architecture from damage. Nowadays, the area is plenty of antique shops, especially along Defensa street, between Independencia and San Juan avenues. This is the perfect place for a walk on Sundays, since there is an antiques fair in Dorrego Square (on the corner of Defensa and Carlos Calvo streets) every Sunday morning, opening at 10 AM. (see p. 35).

San Telmo in 3 dimensions

Lezama Park

It is the highest area along the riverbanks. During the 17th Century, it was used as an area for warehouses and slave cabins. It later became the ranch of the Lezama family and, in 1884, the whole plot was purchased by the city's government and used to build a the park we can visit nowadays. It was restored recently and it houses a sculpture garden and a watchtower.

Bar Británico (Britanic bar)

It is a mythical spot of Buenos Aires, crowded by artists and bohemians, the perfect place for the sleepless, since it is always open. Right across the street you will find Hipopótamus Bar, which is quite similar to the British Bar.

Rusian Orthodox Church

In front of the park you may see the Russian Orthodox Church, an exotic building with five onion-shaped domes erected in the early 20th Century period.

National History Museum (see p. 36).

Av. Caseros

Bolívar

Defensa

Brasil

Av. Juan de Garay

Cochabamba

Au 25 de Mayo

Balcarce

Av. Paseo Colón

Museum of Modern Art: *San Juan 350.*
It houses important painting and sculpture collections of contemporary art, both from Argentina and from abroad. Exhibitions are regularly organized in the Museum. It had many famous directors, it was founded by Rafael Squirru and it gained dynamism and prestige during Raúl Santana's administration, a period during which great exhibitions were held, such as that of the Cobra group. The building used to be a tobacco storehouse and it was restored to serve as a museum.

Opening time:
Monday through Friday from 10 AM to 8 PM. Saturdays, Sundays and Public Holidays from 11 AM to 8 PM.
Guided tours:
for the public in general, Tuesday through Sunday at 5 PM; for institutions: request in advance by phone. Ticket price: $ 1. Wednesdays free in both wings.

Work by Raúl Lozza, Museum's collection.

San Telmo Quarter

San Telmo's Fair

It is held every Sunday from 10 Am to 6 Pm in Dorrego Square and adjoining streets. You may go and purchase antiques or small works of art, or you may just mingle with people and be entertained by street performers and tango dancers.

Forner-Bigatti Foundation

Facing Dorrego Square there is a house that dates from the 1930s, an example of nationalist architecture. It was the place of abode of Raquel Forner and Alfredo Bigatti, two well-known visual artists from Argentina.

Bar Dorrego

Humberto Primo and Defensa st.. It is the most traditional and well-known bar in the area. Inside of the bar you may breathe the atmosphere of a typical tavern of the 1920s.

San Pedro Telmo's Church: *(See P. 35)*

Bolívar

Defensa

Carlos Calvo

San Juan

Humberto Primo

Balcarce

Estados Unidos

Av. Independencia

Av. Paseo Colón

Song for Labor, *sculpture by Rogelio Yrurtia. The author was one of Rodin's disciples and he is known as one of the most important Latin American sculptors. (The work may be seen in the piazza located at the corner of Paseo Colón and Independencia Avenue).*

Former Eva Perón Foundation and current College of Engineering

This building was designed during a military government in the 1930s and it is a typical example of German neoclassical architecture. It was built in the 1940s and it served as the seat of Eva Perón Foundation, the purpose of which was to aid the poor.

33

House of the Ezeiza Family

It was built around 1880 and it has a row of several patios. This kind of buildings were called "sausage houses" in Buenos Aires and they were an Argentinian version of the old Roman Domus as adapted to plots of land that were just 11 meters wide. It also served as a typical tenement house that could hold a maximum of 32 families. It was restored in 1982 and it became a commercial passage. Today, you may find antique shops and souvenir stores that sell posters and cards.

courtyard of the cistern

courtyard of the Tree

María de San Telmo: *store that sells articles for tourists, such as travel guides, posters, cards and souvenirs.*

courtyard of the Time

Church of our Lady of Belén & San Pedro González Telmo

On Humberto I° St. 340.

The construction of the church began in 1734 on the project plan by the jesuit architect brother Andrés Blanqui and the support of the brothers Juan Bautista Prímoli and José Schmidt and who finished the construction was the Italian master Antonio Masella; the last restauration was made by Pelayo Sáinz in 1918. The front was made in eclectic style ,with some architectonic elements of Neo Colonial and Barroc styles and in the upper part St. Peter Gonzalez Telmo´s image has been located. It has been recognized as National Historical Monument.

San Pedro Telmo's Church.

Dome of plant of eight side.

Dome with coating of Stone.

Jesuit Oratory.

Humberto Primo

Porch and facade neoclasic, ended in 1942.

Access to the penitentiary museum.

Courtyard of the 18th century.

Argentine Penitentiary Museum "Antonio Ballvé"

378, Humberto I° St.
The museum is an 1760 building and the plans were made by the architect Antonio Masella. At the first time, it had been the Spiritual Retreat House for men. In 1767, when Jesuit Order was sent off, City Hall established here Women Jail under the supervision of Penitentiary Service until 1978 when the jail was moved to the neighbourhood of Ezeiza. The Our Lady of Carmen Chapel, an 1734 construction, is located inside this museum.

Dorrego Square in 3 dimensions

Dorrego Square:

Between Humberto I, Defensa, Anselmo Aieta and Bethlem Streets.

It was declared of National Historical Interest because this is where the people met to reconfirm their Declaration of Independence from Spain. Dorrego is the oldest square in the city after Plaza de Mayo Sq. On Sundays from 10.00 to 17.00 hs. an Antique Market functions here organized by City Museum, while the Square seems to go back into the past and dancers move to the sound of Tangos and Milongas.

Almacén de Tangos Generales: store that sells posters and souvenirs.

Foundation Forner Bigati. Raquel Forner and Alfredo Bigati were two greit Argentine artists. This house was their shop.

Antique shop specialized in phonographs and old record players on the corner of Bethlen and Defensa streets.

Bethlem

Anselmo Aieta

Defensa

Humberto Primo

Dorrego Bar, on the corner of Defensa and Carlos Calvo streets.

Housing building accomplished by the architects Poblet and Ortuzar of academic style, about 1920s.

Street performers and tango dancers on the corner of Defensa and Carlos Calvo streets.

Lezama Park

Amphitheatre

Av. Paseo Colón

Looking.

Sculptures courtyard.

Av. Martín García

Russian Orthodox Church.

Av. Caseros

Britanic Bar

Av. Brasil

Defensa

National Historical Museum.

Monument Source to Sir Pedro de Mendoza.

Monument to the International fraternity.

National Museum of History

The national Museum of History building used to be the house of the Lezama family. Its appearance is similar to that of an Italian palazzo, with a square-shaped tower that dominated the southern area of the city for many years.

Its 32 rooms made up one of the most important residences during the first half of the 19th Century. In 1897, the building was assigned to the National Museum of History, founded by Adolfo Carranza. The Museum's collection shows us a panoramic view of the history of Argentina since the 16th Century until the end of the 19th Century.

A special room devoted to General San Martín houses a reproduction of his room in Grand Bourg, France. Relics from the Jesuits' missions and trophies from the battle of Suipacha are also on display. The Museum also has an important collection of drawings and paintings by travelling artists of the 19th Century, such as French painter Palliere, Italian artist Pellegrini and French engraver Gericault.

Undoubtedly, the main work of art in this collection is a series of paintings on the War of Paraguay by Cándido López.

Entrance gate with archways in typical Italian style.

Also in the Museum's garden, a collection of cannons and bells from different periods.

Five domes carried in metal.

Crossings watching to the East hold with chains.

Icon of the Santísima Trinidad.

Pulpits.

Choir.

Access staircase to the Shrine that this in the first floor.

Altar watching to the East.

Av. Brasil

Opening times:
Tuesday through Friday, from 2 PM to 6 PM. Saturdays and Sundays from 3 PM to 7 PM. Admission: free.

Russian Orthodox Church of the Holy Trinidad

315 Brasil St. between Defensa and Paseo Colón Streets.

This church was opened in 1904; the original project was made by the architect of Russian Holy Synod, Mihail Preobrazensky, and was adapted by the architect Alejandro Christophersen. The temple was built in Muscovite style of XVII century.

Square-shaped tower that dominates the museum's building.

Detail of a painting by José Bouche that depicts a Spaniard fraternizing with a Native American woman.

Engraving, 1794. It depicts and Argentinian cowboy or "gaucho" catching a cow with his rope.

18th-Century board engraved in the Jesuits' missions.

Defensa

"Review by Río Negro", oil painting by Juan Manuel Blanes.

"Maipú Battle", lithography by Gericault, 1819.

"View of Curuzú", oil painting by Cándido López.

Opening of the first railway system (August 30, 1857).

Oil painting by F. Augero, 1865. Battle between Native Americans and national guard forces.

The origin of this quarter is undoubtedly connected with the Rivulet or Riachuelo, on the banks of which it started to develop.

The activity brought about by the river, the increase in trade, the presence of shipyards and other factors attracted people who settled down in this area of the city. It was not long before emigrants started to move into the quarter. Most of them came from Genoa, in Italy, and therefore, by 1870, la Boca had already acquired its own shape. It still remains as the only part of the city that has a close relationship with the river.

The heart of the quarter is Caminito street, a narrow pedestrian passage almost 100 meters long which was built on an old stretch for rails and took its name from a famous tango song by Juan de Dios Filiberto. The typical houses in this area are made up of formed sheet metal and most of them have become either tenement houses or painters' studios. Their characteristic colorful walls arise from an project designed by painter Benito Quinquela Martín, who thought that painting the walls in different colors would give Caminito a definite character. If you walk along the rivulet's bank, you will come across Nicolás Avellaneda bridge, which offers a full panoramic view of the area and the river. Next to this bridge stands the old transporter bridge, which was built in 1908 and is currently abandoned.

Caminito Street

Bas-relief on popular topics in Caminito Street.

In Caminito street there is an outdoors museum with sculptures, engravings and mural paintings on popular issues. Besides, visual artists offer their small pieces of art for sale at low prices and most of their work focuses on the neighborhood and on tango culture.. In the surrounding area there are lots of souvenir shops.

Opening time
Monday to Sundays: of 9 to 19 hs. Admition Free.

Caminito Street.

Magallanes

Garibaldi

Caminito

Lamadrid

Del Valle Iberlucea

Vuelta de Rocha.

Av. Pedro de Mendoza

Lamadrid

PROA Foundation.
(see p. 42).

(see p. 42).

Handicraft fair.

De la Ribera Theater

RIACHUELO

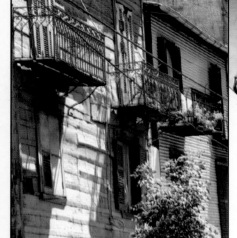

Old Transporter Bridge.

Original houses on the corner of Magallanes and Garibaldi streets.

Nicolas Avellaneda Bridge.

RIACHUELO

Boca Juniors Stadium.

Brandsen

Puerto de Palos

Suárez

Martín Rodríguez

Olavarría

Av. Almirante Brown

La Perla Bar: traditional business in the city, on the corner of Pedro de Mendoza and del Valle Ibarlucea streets.

Voluntary Firemans quarter

In the entrance to Caminito street, you will find street performers and many couples of tango dancers.

San Juan
Evangelista Church

Benito Quinquela Martín School and Museum, located at Pedro de Mendoza 1835.

Old barges and tugboats remain stranded in Vuelta de Rocha, which used to be a dynamic commercial port in front of Caminito.

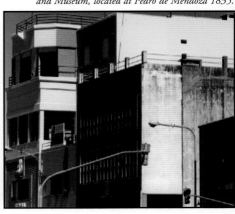

Boca Juniors Soccer Stadium

La Boca quarter is closely related to the history of Boca Juniors Soccer Club, the most popular one in the city. Due to its vertical structure that seems to go beyond the sidewalk's limits, the stadium is called La Bombonera, that is, The Chocolate Box. It can hold barely more than 50,000 spectators.

Near the stadium, on the corner of

Brandsen and Del Valle Iberlucea streets, there are two well-known, excellent restaurants: la Cancha and El Carlitos. Further away from the stadium, in number 64 of Cafarena street, you will find another restaurant called El Obrero.

The area that stretches along Necochea street between Brandsen and Olavarría streets is crowded with canteens that buzz with activity in the evening.

Proa Fundation

It organizes many cultural activities. Its rooms have served as exhibition halls for paintings of major local and international artists, such as German painter and photographer Anselm Kiefer, and Mexican painter Julio Galán.

"While I Wake Up", oil painting by Julio Galán.

Quinquela Martín School and Museum

On the higher floors of Quinquela Martín Elementary School you will find the Museum of Painting and Sculpture. Its founder, Benito Quinquela Martín, intended to show in its great collection not only the work of painters from La Boca but also that of many Argentinian artists from the first half of this Century. Among them, it is worth mentioning Quinquela Martín himself, Fortunato Lacámera, Policastro, Spilimbergo, Victorica, Sívori, Gramajo Guitiérrez and Rodolfo Cascales.

On the third floor of the building, which has a superb watchtower that overlooks Vuelta de Rocha, we will find the apartment where Quinquela Martín worked and lived until the end of his life, in 1972. Upon his death, he left the whole building, including De La Ribera Theater next door, to the city's government.

"Barges", oil painting by Quinquela Martín.

"From my studio", oil painting by Fortunato Lacámera.

Quinquela.   *Filiberto.*   *Lacámera.*

Shop of the painter Quinquela Martin in the 1th finish floor, looking.

Terrace, sculptures exposition.

Rooms of permanent exposition.

room of the Mascarones.

De la Ribera theatre

In the Hall of the theatre there are two important oils of Quinquela.

Opening time: Tuesday through Friday from 8 AM to 5:30 PM. Saturdays and Sundays from 8 AM to 12 and from 1 PM to 5:30 PM. **Admission:** free. **Address:** Pedro de Mendoza 1835.

"The Model", oil painting by Leopoldo Presas.

"The Utopia of my Neighborhood", sculpture by Ricardo Longhand.

"Mirador", acrylic painting by Rómulo Macció.

Nowadays, many painters and sculptors live and work in La Boca, which allows the quarter to preserve its tradition as a neighborhood of artists and bohemians. These are just some samples of those artists' work.

Puerto Madero and Biological Reserve

In 1880, the city's government began to build a new port, which was later given the name Port Madero in honor of Engineer Eduardo Madero, its designer.

The project turned out to be quite similar to that of the docklands in London, with four closed and connected docks which are placed parallel to the river. In 1910, the port was already too small for the needs of a city that had increasingly gained a greater commercial activity. It was then that the so-called New Port (Puerto Nuevo) was built north of Puerto Madero. As years went by, Puerto Madero was abandoned but, in the early 1990s, a redevelopment project was carried out and the whole port became a promenade, with apartments, offices and recreation areas.

In the old redeveloped warehouses you will find a great number of restaurants (quite expensive), movie theaters, drugstores and even a University campus.

We suggest that you take a walk along the docklands. The area is very attractive, both during the day and in the evening.

If you walk along Brasil street towards the river, you will pass by Ernesto de la Cárcova Art School, where you may visit the Museum of Compared Sculpture (see p. 47) and, if you turn left when you get to Costanera Avenue, you will find Las Nereidas Fountain and the Biological Reserve (see p. 47).

Foto: Otilio Moralejo

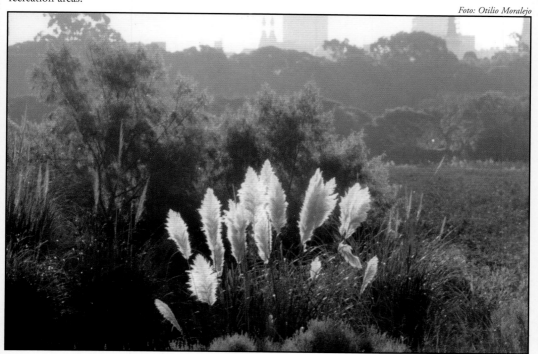

Puerto Madero Dock I and II

*The newly restored
warehouses in Puerto Madero have preserved
their original appearance for the most part.
They are solid buildings made up of clay bricks
in English style and
they house pricey lofts that may be used as either
offices or apartments.*

Museum of tracing and compared Sculpture.

It is inside Ernesto de la Cárcova
Art School. In the museum's rooms
you will find direct reproductions
of the main sculptures in the
history of art. They were
brought to Argentina in
the beginning of this
Century and, among
them, we can mention some
of Michelangelo's pieces
(see David in the picture).
When you visit the museum,
you will also find perfect
tracings of Egyptian relieves.
Finally, we suggest that you
take a walk on the cozy gardens
at the back of the school,
which are plenty of
sculptures and mural
paintings.

Av. Brasil

Av. Garay

Av. San Juan

Juana Manuela Gorriti

Malecom Tower.

Conjunto de cines

Dock I

Pierina Dealessi

Elvira Rawson de Dellepiane

Julieta Lanteri

Av. Calabria

Espigón Plus Ultra

*Las Nereidas Fountain: It is the work of sculptor
Lola Mora, who designed it in the city of Rome
in 1902.
Its first location was in the downtown area, but
due to the scandal caused by the nude figures, it
was moved to its current location in 1918. The
material used is Carrara marble. Tritons, Nereids
and an Aphrodite-Venus make up a harmonious
sculptural work.*

Puerto Madero and Biological Reserve

Av. Primo
Carlos Calvo
Balcarce
Estados Unidos
Av. Independencia
Chile
Mexico
Venezuela
Av. Belgrano

Av. Ingeniero Huergo

Av. Alicia Moreau de Justo

Universidad Católica

Bvd. Rosario Vera Peñaloza

Dock II

Bvd. Azucena Villaflor

Dock III

Olga Cossettini
E. Escurra
Petrona Eyle
Macacha Güemes
Pierina Dealessi
Bvd. Azucena Villaflor
Azucena Marza
Marta Lynch

Juana Manso

Aime Paine
F. Escurra

Bvd. Azucena Villaflor
Av. de los Italianos

Av. Calabria

Av. Costanera Dr. Tristan Achaval Rodriguez

Newsletter BuildingEl
Porteño:
*reciclated for the famous
designer Philipe Starck.*

Del Faro Tower

De los Coipos lake

Pérgola Luis Viale

Museum of Telecommunications: In the
1930s, it was a beer pub built by
Hungarian Modernist architect Andres
Kalnay and it became a museum in 1979.

Biological Reserve: *Una de las
entradas está junto al espigón frente
a la fuente de Las Nereidas. Al
rellenar el río con demoliciones de
edificios de la ciudad, se fue
conformando un ecosistema similar al
existente antes de la fundación de la
ciudad. Hay una rica fauna icticola,
variedad de patos silvestres, nutrias y
otros pequeños animales, es una
oportunidad para pasear por la pampa
a pocos metros del centro de la ciudad.*

Puerto Madero Dock III and IV

If we keep walking along Puerto Madero, we will reach Docks III and IV, where the best restaurants are located. Sarmiento Frigate is anchored just a few steps from there and it is open for visitors. In the area of Docks III and IV you will see modern monumental buildings.

Once you have left Puerto Madero, you may continue walking along L. N. Alem avenue, an area where you will notice many different architectural styles. This part of the city is called El Bajo or The Downward Area. In La Recova neighborhood, which runs along L. N. Alem avenue, you will find several good-quality, inexpensive restaurants.

Office Building for the Department of the Army.

Vista Edificios de la City desde Puerto Madero.

Puerto Madero and Biological Reserve

Edificio de la Bolsa de Comercio.

Building Comega.

Luna Park Stadium

Edificio del Diario "La Nación", uno de los más importantes de habla hispana.

ALAS Building

Perón

Sarmiento

Av. Corrientes

Reconquista

Lavalle

Tucumán

Av. Córdoba

Av. Leandro N. Alem

Roma Garden

Viamonte

Rosales

Bouchard

Av. Eduardo Madero

Palacio del Correo Argentino: Recomendamos visitar los halls de planta baja y primer piso.

Av. Alicia Moreau de Justo

Oficina de Información Turística

Edificio Telecom.

Dock IV

Museo de arte fundación Fortabat.

Yatching Club

Bvd. Cecelia Grierson

Ferry a Colonia y Montevideo

Pierina Dealessi

Emma de la Barra

R. Paccini de Alvear

Enriquta Sanchez de Thompson

Opera Bay

Victoria Ocampo

Juana Manso

Av. de los Italianos

Yatch Club Argentino

Av. Costanera Intendente Carlos Noel

Biological Reserve

Sarmiento Frigate was a training ship for the Argentine Navy. It sailed innumerable times around the world. Nowadays, it is a museum anchored in dock 3.

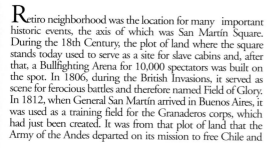

Peru. The estate was finally turned into a square and named after General San Martín in 1878, for the 100th anniversary of the hero's birth.

The current landscape was designed in 1883 by French architect and landscape designer Carlos Thays. The square is on a gentle slope and on the sunny days of the year, it suddenly becomes a sunbathing spot. At the base of the slope, there stands a memorial to the soldiers that died during the war in our Malvinas (Falkland Islands) in 1982.

In the surrounding area of the square, you will find many important buildings, such as the Kavanagh (see p. 50) the Plaza Hotel, the Military Club building and San Martín Palace.

Florida street leads into the square and on its last blocks you may find many stores and shopping centers. If you walk across L.N. Alem avenue, you will reach a modern urban complex called Catalinas Norte, the most imposing group of buildings in the whole city (see p. 51). In the square's surrounding area there is a lot of cultural activity and an exciting nightlife. It is in this area that you will find the main Art Galleries in the city as well as many ethnic food restaurants and fashionable bars.

Retiro neighborhood was the location for many important historic events, the axis of which was San Martín Square. During the 18th Century, the plot of land where the square stands today used to serve as a site for slave cabins and, after that, a Bullfighting Arena for 10,000 spectators was built on the spot. In 1806, during the British Invasions, it served as scene for ferocious battles and therefore named Field of Glory. In 1812, when General San Martín arrived in Buenos Aires, it was used as a training field for the Granaderos corps, which had just been created. It was from that plot of land that the Army of the Andes departed on its mission to free Chile and

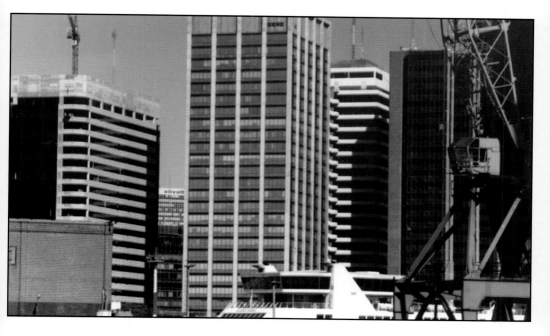

Retiro y Plaza San Martín Square in 3 dimensions

Military Club (Paz Palace): It was opened in 1925 and, for the time, it had a clearly academic and decadent style. It bears some resemblance with the Louvre Palace in Paris. It used to be part of a group of similar mansions that stretched along Santa Fe avenue and its surrounding area.

National Parks Service: It is one of the oldest residences that stand in the area. It was built in 1880.

National Weapons Museum: It is in the same building as the Military Club, but the entrance door to the museum is at number 745, Marcelo T. de Alvear street. **Opening time:** Wednesday through Friday, 3 PM to 7 PM. Admission: $ 1.

Entrance gate to the Military Club building, wrought iron and bronze.

Florida street where it meets Paraguay Street.

Libertador Hotel

Navy Club, (see p. 54).

Pacific Galleries or "Galerías Pacífico" (see p. 54).

Catalinas Convent, (see p. 54).

Claridge Hotel.

Alas Building, on Leandro N. Alem street.

52

Retiro / Plaza San Martín Square

Monument to General San Martín: It stands right across Santa Fe avenue and it was the first equestrian monument in the country. It was created in 1862 by French sculptor Luis José Daumas.

San Martín Palace: It is one of the seats of the Argentinian Department of State.

Kavanagh Building: It was designed in 1935 by architects Sanchez, Lagos and De La Torre. It is 120 meters high and it once was the tallest building in South America and the first one built with reinforced concrete. Its unevenly shape was a symbol of the city for a long period.

Tuncal

Basavilbaso

Av. del Libertador

Estación
de Retiro

Av. del Libertador

Plaza

Tower of the British

Plaza Hotel (see p. 55).

Av. Leandro N. Alem

Sheraton Hotel .

Monument to the arrears in the war of Malvinas in the year 1982.

Basilica of the Blessed Sacrament. (see p. 55)

Catalinas Norte Urban Complex

53

Galerías Pacífico
Borges Cultural Center in 3 dimensions

The building covers most of the area bound by Córdoba avenue, Florida street, San Martín street and Viamonte street. It was erected in the late 19th Century by architect Levacher for the purpose of housing a market called Au Bon Marché. Its designer took as a model a gallery in Milan called Vittorio Emanuelle II. After that, the building was given several purposes; it was even part of the National Museum of Fine Arts from 1896 to 1910. In the 1940s, it underwent a deep change, which altered its original appearance. From that time, there remain the excellent frescoes painted by Antonio Berni, Lino Spilimbergo, Castagnino and Colmeiro. In the 1960s, the building started to deteriorate gradually due to a lack of proper maintenance services. It was not until 1989 that restoration measures were adopted.

Nowadays, the building serves as buzzing shopping center with three stories, a big restaurant area and a movie theater.

Santa Catalina de Siena Church and Convent: The Convent was opened in 1745, it was sacked during the British Invasions and is currently empty. The Church is quite small and it has only one nave. It has been declared to be a Historical Monument.

Navy Club: It was built in 1941 and it has many richly ornamented halls. Its entrance door, on the corner of Florida street and Córdoba avenue, is entirely carved in bronze, what makes it undoubtedly magnificent. (See picture)

Santa Catalina de Siena Church and Convent: *The Convent was opened in 1745, it was sacked during the British Invasions and is currently empty. The Church is quite small and it has only one nave. It has been declared to be a Historical Monument.*

Center Navy Building

Av. Córdoba

San Martín

Calle Florida hacia Plaza San Martín

Calle Florida hacia Plaza de Mayo

Entrance door to the Navy Club.

Viamonte

Interior of Galerías Pacífico (formerly, Au Bon Marché).

Detail of the fountain and the mural paintings in the central area of Galerías Pacífico.

Entrance door to Galerías Pacífico on Viamonte street.

Kavanagh Building, Basilic of the blessed Sacrament and Marriott Hotel Plaza

It was opened in 1936, and for many years, it was the highest framework of reinforced concrete of South America. It was built by decision of Corina Kavanagh, this building of 120 metres, reduces in a gradual way the area of its floors, according to the rules of the codigo de edificación (building code) and ends in several terraces gardens. It was designed by the architects Sanchez, Lagos and De la Torre. It was built during 14 months and the front shows elements of the rationalist architecture, this style characterized the constructions of the 30s. The hotel Marriot Plaza is

Kavanagh Building.

Basilica of the Sacrament Holy.

Private Passage.

San Martín

Acceso a la cripta.

Florida

Marcelo T. de Alvear

Custody of the Sacrament Holy.

Marriot Plaza Hotel.

Borges Cultural Center: The same building that houses Galerías Pacífico serves as the seat for Borges Cultural Center. If you enter the building through the door on the corner of Viamonte and San Martín streets and walk upstairs to the second floor on the wide staircase, you will get to a series of halls that house different exhibitions. The Cultural Center also has a library, an interactive room for children and a big auditorium.

It is open from Monday through Sunday, 10 AM to 8 PM.

View of an exhibition hall on the second floor of Borges Cultural Center.

separated through a private passage, designed with the purpose of not obstructing the view from the square of the front of the Basilica del Santisimo Sacramento. It was considered a jewel of the architectonic ecclesiastical art, this church was designed by the architects Coulomb and Chauvert, then it was modified by Ernesto Vespegnani.

It was built because of the generosity of Mrs Mercedes Castellano de Anchorena, her remains are in the cryp. Its eclectic front shows reminiscense of the gothic, byzantine and romantic style and it is highlighted the

sculptural group that represents the devout, julian eymard-founder of the religious group-together with two angels on their knees, made in marble.

Marriot Plaza Hotel is the most stylish and exquisite building of Buenos Aires. It was designed by the architect Alfred Zucker and opened in 1909. It is a progressive work for that period. The front is highlighted and characteristics of the german baroque are shown. It has been reformed and enlarged several times throughout the years and many politicians, sportmen or sport-women and people from the world-wide show stayed there.

Cultural areas, restaurants and bars in Retiro in 3 dimensions

The area bound by San Martín Square, Santa Fé avenue, Córdoba avenue, L.N. Alem avenue and Maipú street was the core of bustling cultural activity during the 1960s, which was encouraged by numerous cultural institutions located there. The most important ones among those institutions were Di Tella Institute and, by the end of the 1970s, the CAYC (Center for Art and Communication). However, the area is also plenty of art galleries an bars which, together with these Institutions, helped create a sort of Argentinian SoHo that has only survived in part. Among the bars that were opened in those times, we can mention Bar Baro, on Tres Sargentos alley, and Florida Garden, at the corner of Florida and Paraguay streets. Both on San Martín street and on 25 de Mayo street, a group of post-modern and Irish bars and pubs have come up. They are all buzzing with activity in the evening, which creates a sophisticated and pleasant atmosphere. We suggest that you talk a walk in the area on Saturday morning and in the evening. (See pictures)

Bar Baro, meeting point for artist and intellectuals. Tres Sargentos 415.

El Salmón, restaurant. Reconquista 1014.

Druid, Irish pub. Reconquista 1040.

The Kilkenny, Irish Pub, Marcelo T. de Alvear 399.

Av. del Libertador

Av. Leandro N. Alem

Luisa Pedrouzo Art Gallery

Juncal

Ono Sushi Bar, sushi, restaurante bar. San Martín 974.

Esmeralda   Arenales

Filo, restaurant and pizza house. Art Gallery. San Martín 975.

Av. Santa Fe

Kelly's, presents.

Rubbers Art Gallery.

Marcelo T. de Alvear

San Martín

Reconquista

Klemm Art Gallery M. T. de Alvear 636

Paraguay

Catalinas Restaurant, Lancaster Hotel. Reconquista 850.

Maipú

Galería del Este, book-store- Antique Shop.

Cantina China Maipú 967

Av. Córdoba

Lotus, Thai food. Tres Sargentos 427

House of Borges Maipú 994

Galería Larreta, design "diseñadores del bajo" Florida 1000.

ICI "Institute of Iberoamerican Cooperation". Library, auditorium and Art Gallery. Florida 943.

Florida

Galería del Sol, Florida 866.

Florida Garden, Bar. Corner of Florida and Paraguay street.

Bar Dadá, meeting point for artist and intellectuals. San Martín 943.

Borges. Foto de Sara Facio.

Ruth Benzacar
Art Gallery. Florida 1000.

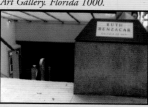

Ruth Benzacar Art Gallery houses an important collection of contemporary Argentinian paintings, among which we should mention many works by Berni.

"Lunch", Tempera painting by Antonio Berni

"Fitz Roy Dolphin" by L.F. Benedit

"Mirrored little worm", oil painting by De La Vega

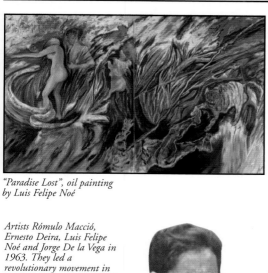

"Paradise Lost", oil painting by Luis Felipe Noé

Artists Alberto Greco, Egle Martin and Marta Minujín in Buenos Aires, 1964.

Artists Rómulo Macció, Ernesto Deira, Luis Felipe Noé and Jorge De la Vega in 1963. They led a revolutionary movement in Argentinian art in the 1960s.

Building of National Parks
Peace Palace

The Edificio de Parques Nacionales belonged to Villar and Haedo families and it was built by the architects Passeron and Brizuela by the of the 19th century in Neo-gothic style. Another building that shows a luxurious and architectonic style is the Circulo Militar that was built at the beginning of the century. It belonged to the family of Jose C. Paz, the founder of La Prensa newspaper. The building was designed by the french architect Louis Sortais. In 1938, it was acquired by the Circulo Militar. It houses the National Museum of Arms where an overview of the worldwide weapons throughout the years is shown.

Anchorena Palace
Chancery

The Palacio San Martin, where the ceremonies of the foreign affairs ministry are currently held, was the residence of Anchorena family until 1936. The plan was designed by the architect Alejandro Cristophersen for Mercedes Castellanos de Anchorena and her children. It is only one building with three independent residences connected to a central hall. The distinctive eclecticism of Christophersen can be seen here and there is a combination of elements of the French Academicism and Bourbon style. It is important to highlight the front of the new location of "Cancilleria", A "Curtain wall" seeking to have a dialogue with Palacio San Martin through the image reflected in the windows and ending in a doubtless post-modernist connection.

If you walk north on Esmeralda street from San Martín Square to Juncal street, you will find Estrogamou Palace (see p. 55). Arroyo street, with its art galleries and antiques shops starts there. This winding street finishes at Carlos Pellegrini Square, across 9 de Julio avenue. This little Parisian corner is surrounded by luxury houses, out of which the Brazilian and French Embassies and the Jockey Club stand out. These houses were built during the first decades of the 20th Century and they remind us of an opulent country, which at the time was called the "granary of the world".

The heads of the families who used to own these buildings were wealthy landowners in La Pampa. In building their houses, they forgot their taste for colonial architecture and gave the city a set of French-style mansions in an effort to imitate European aristocracy. Most of these buildings were designed by architects Rene Sergent, Lanus, Harry and Cristopherssen.

Retiro and Alvear Avenue in 3 d

Duhau Residence and Apostolic Nunciature: They make up a well-matching group of 3 mansions on Alvear avenue. The Apostolic Nunciature was built by architect Le Monnier and it served as residence for popes Pius XII and John Paul II during their visits to Buenos Aires.

Del Infinito Art Gallery.

Carlos Pellegrini Square: Undoubtedly, it is the most French-styled square you will find in Buenos Aires. It is surrounded by a large group of examples of rationalist architecture built during the 1930s. The central area of the square is crowned by a monument to Dr Carlos Pellegrini, former Argentinian President. The Jockey Club, a prestigious institution that follows the style of the most exclusive English clubs, lies in front of the square. It has a huge and valuable library.

Brazil Embassy.

Detail of the top floor in Lenguas Vivas School. It stands on Carlos Pellegrini avenue, across from Hyatt Hotel.

French Embassy: Former Ortiz-Basualdo residence. It was built in 1912 by French architect Paul Pater.

Atica Art Gallery. Libertad 1240

Arroyo Street: It is one of the few winding streets in the city, which gives it a nice and singular appearance. It is crowded with art galleries and antique shops, Palatina being the most traditional one among them.

Painting by Octavio Pinto, one of the most important landscape painters in Argentina. Some of his pieces may be seen in the back hall of Palatina art gallery.

Principium Art Gallery. Esmeralda 1357

Patio Bullrich: It is a classy shopping center. Inside of it, you may find some traces of the old, renovated building, which used to serve as location for livestock auctions. It has an entrance door on Posadas street and another one on Libertador avenue. In the building, there is a movie theater and some sophisticated restaurants, such as Cipriani, on Posadas street.

Posadas

Caesar Park Hotel.

Four Season Hotel

Av. del Libertador

Museum of Spanish-American Art Isaac Fernandez Blanco

The former Nöel Palace is currently the seat for our Museum of Spanish-American Art. It was built in the 1920s by architect Martin Nöel, founder of the neocolonial architectural style. The main building, surrounded by gardens, has balconies with closings and fences in wrought iron. It houses the museum's pieces, among which we can mention a colonial silverware collection that is thought to be the most important one in the continent. The library is an interesting spot with its baroque boiserie, where valuable religious objects are on exhibition. The gardens make the perfect place to relax among the high-rise apartment buildings in the area. The Museum is located at Suipacha 1422.

Restaurants on Posadas Street and 9 de Julio Avenue:
from Hyatt Hotel, under the highway, the main Argentinian gourmets have opened their restaurants to offer different kinds of food to the public. The services are quite expensive. Across the street from the restaurant area, you will find Zurbarán Gallery, one of the main art galleries in the city specialized in Argentinian art.

Opening time: Tuesday through Sunday, 2 PM to 7 PM. Admission: $ 2.

Folkloric engraving dating from the early 19th Cent.

Arroyo Street: Area de galerías de arte y anticuarios. Entre otras Galería Palatina, Zabaleta Lab, Mercedes Pinto, Agustina del Campo, Galería Arroyo, Praxis y Principium; Los viernes por la noche se organiza el Galery Nights con gran concurrencia de público.

Av. del Libertador

Mercedes Pinto
Art Gallery
Arroyo y Suipacha
Arroyo Gallery

Sofitel Hotel.
Bar and restorant.
Arroyo 845

Arroyo
Art Gallery.
Arroyo 830

Estrugamou Palace,
It was built in 1922 by architects Sauze and Mouguier. It is a apartment building with suites covering 500 to 600 square meters. The building material was exported from France and, if you peer into the entrance hall, you will find a bronze reproduction of the Victory of Samothrace, a treasure of the Louvre in Paris.

Alvear Avenue in 3 dimensions

First called Bella Vista, Alvear Avenue was designed in 1885 through Buenos Aires' first Mayor, Don Torcuato de Alvear's initiative, in honour to his father, Carlos Maria de Alvear. It starts in front of Carlos Pellegrini's Monument and Piazza and ends in front of Mayor Torcuato de Alvea'r's.

The Monument inaugurated in 1900 was made by Juan Lauer and consists of a marble column in Doric style at the top of which is a winged figure representing "Glory"("La Gloria").In its middle section where the shaft is placed we find the national hero's bust. On its base 3 bas-reliefs are found representing "The Opening up of Avenida de Mayo" ("La apertura de la avenida de mayo"), "The City's Pavement" ("La Pavimentacion de la Ciudad") and "Recoleta Repairs" ("Arreglo de la Recoleta) all of which remind us of Torcuato de Alvear's progressive ideas about city and urban development. On both sides of Alvear Avenue stand beautiful homes and residences like Pereda Family Palace (at present the Embassy of Brazil), Ortiz Basualdo Family Residence (French Embassy) and Concepcion Unzue de Casares Palace (at present the Jockey Club premises) and the Residences of Atucha and Alzaga Unzue Families which are now integrated to the Hyatt Hotel.

The above mentioned buildings lead to Carlos Pellegrini Piazza where Alvear Avenue finds its urban axis and limits all excelling in their French architecture bringing about an unprecedented Parisian image.

At the intersection of Alvear Avenue and Ayacucho we find Alvear Palace Hotel, one of of our finest expressions in hotel services. Built in 1928 by Engineer Escudero y Ortuzar and Architects Valentin Brodski and Estanislao Pirovano its 11 floors and 280 rooms, decorated in different styles, show great comfort and high quality expressions of finesse and good taste.

The top floor Roof Garden and terraces offer a wonderful view of the river and surounding buildings. Many famous worldwide figures, Presidents from foreign countries, diplomats, artists, musicians and professionals have stayed at Alvear Palace Hotel which today still keeps its traditional charme.

Hyatt Hotel

Brazil Embassy

French Embassy

Alzaga Unzue Palace

Caesar Park Hotel

Arroyo

Libertad

Av. Alvear

Carlos Pellegr. Square

Parera

Jockey Club

Montevideo

Hotel

Sothebys

Apostolic Nunciature

Duhau Palace

Rodriguez Peña

Culture Secretary

Alvear Hotel

Av. Callao

Av. Alvear

Ayacucho

Schiaffino

Alvear Square.

Atucha Palace

Alzaga Unsué Palace

La Recoleta area

People started to settle down in this area in 1870, when the cholera and yellow fever plagues brought wealthy families from the southern areas of the city to the north region.

The neighborhood acquired a sumptuous appearance in 1885, when Alvear avenue was built and mansions, squares and parks started to come up along it.

Behind the Church of Recoleta, there used to be an area covered with slaughterhouses and stockyards, where carts coming from the northern zones of the country would stop. It served as a meeting point for country laborers and outcasts and it was in this environment, plenty of cafeterias, general stores and tenement houses that tango music is thought to have been born. This is the place where the mythical Armenonville was located, on the corner of Libertador avenue and Tagle street. This and the Palais de Glace were the main tango ballrooms in the country.

Out tour, which comes from Alvear avenue in Retiro, will take us left to San Martín de Tours Park, a lovely place full of enormous magnolia trees. If we walk across the park to our right, we will find the cemetery, the Church of Pilar and the Recoleta Cultural Center. After that, if we walk across Francia Square, we will reach the National Museum of Fine Arts and further along a tree-covered Libertador avenue, we will find the National Library and the Museum of Decorative and Eastern Arts.

In the early 18th Century, the Recoleta area used to be an impassable mount where bandits and crooks would seek refuge. The first Franciscan Chapel and Convent was built in the period ranging from 1716 to 1730 and it served as a retreat for the Order of Franciscans, who had their main church in the city's central area. These churches, located in the outskirts of the city, used to be called Recoletas and the monks who lived there were the Recoletos, which gave its name to this area of Buenos Aires.

Recoleta area in 3 dimensions

Basilica of our lady of Pilar

Construction began in 1716 and the church was consecrated in 1732. Its harmonious facade with pilasters and cornices is crowned by a discreet tympanum and a lateral tower that reaches 30 meters high. Inside the church you will find just one nave surrounded by niches where the smaller altars are placed. The main altarpiece was brought from northern Peru and it has a wrought-silver frontal made by Native Americans from Jujuy. The church also has a lot of interesting religious icons, such as the Christ of Humility and Patience, a Crucified Christ by sculptor Martínez Montañés, and one of the few images of San Francisco de Paola which have remained in the city.

Building of the Car Argentine Club.

Intendente Alvear Square:

It is located across from the Church of Pilar. If we walk across this square, we will run into Ortiz pedestrian walk, along which there are several restaurants. Going to la Biela for some coffee in the evening is a must. The hundred-year-old rubber plant in the square is the biggest one in the city. Its crown is over 70 meters wide and the tree itself is over 20 meters high. The tree's scientific name is Ficus macrophylla and it was brought from Australia. The square has recently been renovated and, during the weekend, it serves as a huge outdoors theater plenty of mimes, tango dancers and street performers.

Also in the weekend you will find a handicrafts market where you will have the opportunity to purchase pieces made by the best craftsmen at a low price.

La Biela Café, on the corner of Quintana and Ortiz streets.

Engineering Faculty.

Village Recoleta, cine and restaurants. Bookshop, bar Cúspide.

Cementery of the Recoleta

Loi Suite Hotel, restaurant, bar.
Vicente López 1955
Tel.: 5777-8950

Restaurants on Ortiz pedestrian walk, Between Quintana and Guido street.

It is on the left side of the Church and it originally was the Convent's garden and orchard. In 1822, engineer Felipe Bertres designed the plans for a new cemetery in the northern area of the city. In 1828, Governor Manuel Dorrego made the cemetery bigger till it reached its current size. Along the cemetery's streets, you will find mausoleums with sculptures by famous local and international artists. Many well-known people are buried here, such as Eva Duarte de Perón, Domingo Faustino Sarmiento, Juan Manuel de Rosas, Facundo Quiroga and Bartolomé Mitre.

La Recoleta area

National Museum of Decorative and Eastern Arts (see pages 72 and 73).

Bustamante

Peruano Lucena

National Library (see pages 70 and 71).

Tagle

Av. del Libertador

Austria

Av. Figueroa Alcorta

Aguero

National Museum of Fine Arts (see pages 68 and 69)

Av. del Libertador

Av. Figueroa Alcorta

Posadas

Alvear Hotel

Recoleta Cultural Center (see p. 66 y 67).

San Martin de Tours Park, it has an area covered by magnolia trees.

Statue of General Mitre, the terrace around it works as a perfect watchtower.

Monument given by the French government to the Argentinian government, located in front of the Museum of Fine Arts.

University of layers

Monument to Brigadier General Carlos M. de Alvear

It was created by French sculptor Emile Antoine Bourdelle and it is one of the most interesting equestrian statues in the city. It was unveiled in 1925. There are many pieces by the same artist scattered around the park across the street from this monument.

"The Wounded Centaur" by Antoine Bourdelle.

Palais de Glace, Art Center

"Torso" by sculptor Fernando Botero.

Recoleta Cultural Center in 3 dimensions

This building was originally meant to be a Franciscan Convent and it was designed in the middle-18th Century period by Brother Blanqui.

In 1858, it was enlarged and renovated by Juan Buschiazzo and, after that, it became a house for beggars and older people. The people who lived in this house were evicted in 1979 and the building became a Cultural center.

The second renovation project was undertaken by architects Clorindo Testa, Luis Benedit and Jaques Bedel.

If you walk down the entrance hall to your right, you will get to the old cloisters, which surround three patios in a row. Doing this will allow you to visit part of the original building. This area is currently devoted to exhibitions that are regularly renewed. At the end of the long corridor you will find a room where experimental theater plays are usually performed.

If you walk through the patio in front of the entrance hall, you will find three special exhibition halls. One of them is called Cronopios and the other two adjoining rooms have recently been renovated, provided with equipment and conditioned. These are the halls where exhibitions by professional artists from Argentina and from abroad are usually held. There is also an auditorium right where the old chapel used to be, which was adapted to the needs of modern show halls. On the first floor, there is an interactive science museum for children. Visiting the cultural center will be an interesting experience, no matter what day of the week you do it. You will always find it buzzing with activity and shows, as well as the square in front of the entrance hall.

Behind the cultural center, you will see the Hard Rock Café, which has its entrance door on Pueyrredón avenue.

If you walk along the path that is covered with trees to the right of the cultural center, you will get to a restaurant promenade where a wide range of food services is offered. Finally, if you go down on the comfortable escalator, you will enter "Buenos Aires Design", a shopping center exclusively devoted to furniture, household appliances and design objects.

View of the exhibition halls with the original vaulted ceiling

Tank Patio.

Cistern Patio.

Exhibition Halls

Entrance stairway to the first floor.

Fountain Patio

Church of Pilar

View of the O.A.S. Building

Orange Trees Patio

View of the Recoleta Cultural Center facade and entrance door.

Linden Trees Patio

Entrance door to Cronopios hall and Interactive Science Museum.

View of the old chapel (today, an auditorium).

Many people visit the exhibitions during the weekend.

Hard Rock Cafe building

Entrance to Buenos Aires Design

Totem, Sculpture by Hernan Dompe

Window to the Fountain Patio

"UVO" oil painting on canvass by Enzo Cuchi

View of the restaurant area

"The Wings of Desire", acrylic on canvass by Carlos Gorriarena

National Museum of Fine Arts in 3 dimensions

"Typical Orchestra" by Antonio Berni

In 1930, architect Bustillo adapted the building that used to house the water pumps of the city so that it would become the current seat for the National Museum of Fine Arts. This museum covers an area of over 10,000 square meters and it has over 10,000 works of art in its collection. It houses a permanent exhibition in which you may appreciate the most important and exhaustive collection of Argentinian sculpture and painting from the 19th and 20th Centuries. On the ground floor, you will find European paintings from every period, sculptures, paintings and tapestries from the pre-Renaissance period, the Renaissance period and the 17th, 18th and 19th Centuries. This also includes a wide range of impressionist and post-impressionist pieces.

The most important works are a series of war scenes by Goya, "The Surprised Nymph" by Manet, "The Crucifixion" by Lucas Cranach, a portrait attributed to Rembrandt, and other paintings by El Greco, Titian, Gauguin, an excellent Picasso, some works by Modigliani, Tapies, Saura, Sironi, etc.

"The Small Dove" by Ramón Gomez Cornet, 1946

Second Floor:
Direction, Administrative Offices and temporary exhibitions.

Temporary Exhibitions Wing

First Floor:
Argentinian Art, 19th and 20th Centuries

"Figure" by Lino Enea Spilimbergo, 1938

"Processional Crucifix" anonymous in gold, bronze and crystal, 18th Century

"Secretary" by Titian Vecelli

"Portrait of Sister" by Rembrandt van Rijn

"Landing of the Curuzú Troops" by Cándido López

Recoleta area

Untitled, by Antonio Seguí, 1987

"The Surprised Nymph" by Edouard Manet

"The Lady of the Sea" by Paul Gauguin

"On the road two" by Juan Carlos Distéfano, 1980

Temporary Exhibitions Wing

Edgar Degas, "Amarillo y Rosa"

Down floor:
European art,
Century XVI, XVII, XVIII, XIX, XX.

"The Crucifixion of Christ" by Lucas Cranach

"Female Bust" by Amadeo Modigliani

"The Kiss" by Auguste Rodin

National Library

Across the street from the library, you will find a wide extension of parks

It is located on the plot of land of the former Presidential Residence, where its last inhabitant, Eva Perón, passed away.

Construction of the library started in the 1950s and, after many delays and difficulties, it was finally opened in 1992. The building was designed by architects Clorindo Testa, Bullrich and Cazaniga. It is situated in the center of a huge garden and it has entrance doors on Austria street and Agüero street. The building's basis is an enormous esplanade from which you can enjoy a bird's eye view of Libertador avenue and the adjoining parks.

The book storage area is located under this esplanade. It has three underground levels and it may store up to 5 million copies. An elevator will take you to the exhibition hall and the reading room, an immense suite two stories high with magnificent views of the city.

On the first underground level, you will find a valuable collection of national and local newspapers and magazines. The reading room is spacious and informal.

The old library used to be located on México street, in San Telmo quarter (see p. 27) and it was founded in 1810. Jorge Luis Borges was director of the National Library between the 1950s and the 1970s. The new library organizes a wide variety of events, both in its exhibition hall and in the auditorium it houses.

Direction and Administrative Offices

Elevators

Library building as seen from Libertador avenue.

Map Collection.

Reading Room.

Exhibition Hall.

Jorge Luis Borges
Auditorium

Entrance doors

Newspaper and
Magazine Collection

Book storage area

Esplanade

National Museum of Art Deco in 3 dimensions

Facade of the museum as seen from Libertador Av.

Rococo-inspired entrance door.

"View of Rome", oil painting by Jean B. Corot

Pereyra Lucena

Av. del Libertador

N ational Museum of Decorative and Eastern Arts in 3 Dimensions Palace Errázuriz houses the National Museum of Decorative and Eastern Arts. The project was developed by prestigious French architect Rene Sergent, who never visited Buenos Aires and yet designed most of the best mansions in the city, such as those of the Alvear family and Ernesto Bosch's. The building is designed in a French style typical of the late 18th Century period and it reminds us of the chateaux that make up the Place de la Concorde in Paris. You may enter the museum through a wrought iron and bronze entrance gate in Louis XVI style. Once inside of the building, you will find a series of halls that have been decorated in different styles from different periods. Thus, in the first place you will find the entrance patio in Louis XVI style, then you will enter the huge reception hall in Renaissance style, a suite that has unique dimensions (20 meters long, 18 meters wide and over 10 meters high). This hall has been decorated by Nelson. Pay special attention to the magnificent fireplace and the immense windows on its sides.

Other interesting rooms in the museum are the greenhouse and the Regencia hall.

The permanent exhibition displays valuable pieces from the museum's collection, including 18th Century objects, sculptures and paintings. The museum also organizes special events and exhibitions.

Wrought iron and bronze entrance gate in Louis XVI style.

The countess of the Caves of Saw, oil of Anglada Camarassa.

Entrance hall decorated by Nelson. View of the magnificent fireplace carved in stone.

Louis XVI bureau and Chinese vases in Kang Hi style.

"Faint of the Virgin", Flemish carving, 15th Century.

Bustamante

"Virgin and Child with St John Baptist" Renaissance oil painting on wood by Jacopo dell'Sellaio

Museum of Eastern Arts

The Museum of Eastern Arts is located on the first floor of the building and it has many valuable collections of pottery, lacquerwork, engravings and furniture.

In the entrance to the museum you will find a cozy restaurant-bar with an excellent atmosphere. On the main house's basement, you will find a bookshop and souvenir store.

The museum's address is Av. del Libertador 1902 and it is open from Monday through Friday, 3 PM to 7 PM.

"Virgin Mary" polychrome carving, 14th Century.

Guided Tours: Wednesday through Saturday, 3 PM to 6 PM.
Admission: $ 2.

Palermo Neighborhood

In the early 17th Century, the northern area of the city was covered by lowlands and swamps that were easily flooded. A Sicilian man called Juan Palermo bought this land for agricultural purposes and he gave it the name of "Palermo Fields". It was only later, around 1820, that these premises were acquired by Rosas and annexed to the adjoining lands he already possessed. In these fields he built a huge colonial house and he surrounded it with cages that housed exotic animals, which he designed to impress and entertain his visitors. This way, he gave birth to a style that would be imitated by many South American dictators and caudillos.

In 1872, under the initiative of President Sarmiento, Tres de Febrero Park was founded. The complex was made up of a series of gardens: a zoo, a botanical garden, a rose garden and the so-called Palermo Woods, decorated with artificial lakes. Undoubtedly, this is the greatest green area in the city and it will allow us to take a long walk in close contact with nature. There is a wide variety of trees and plants from different parts of the country, some hidden corners and gazebos next to the lakes are undoubtedly charming. We suggest you take this tour on a special sunny day and go to the Planetarium and the Sívori Museum.

Palermo in 3 dimensions

Museo Sívori

It is an important museum of Argentinian painting, sculpture, engraving and illustration from the 19th and 20th Centuries. Its huge collection is only partly exhibited in this newly opened branch. Temporary exhibitions are also held in this museum. It is located at Av de la Infanta 555.

Opening time:
Tuesday through Friday,
12 to 6 PM.

"The Spirit Lamp", oil painting by Marcia Schvartz.

"José León Pagano, bronce", 1936

The Rose Gardens
You may get to the rose gardens either walking along an avenue surrounded by flowerbeds or crossing a bridge upon the lake. There are many interesting spots in the rose gardens, such as the Poet's Corner, the Andalucian Patio, the roses area and a magnificent gazebo that looks upon the lake. These gardens are plenty of visitors during the weekend.

Gimnasia and Esgrima Club

Av. Infanta Isabel

Av. Libertador

Le Parc Tower: it is currently the highest building in the city.

Paseo de la Infanta
the archways formed by the railways viaduct were nicely adapted and renovated so as to become an entertainment area where fashionable discos and restaurants create a great night life.

Palermo Lake

The Rose Garden

The Poet's Corner

Residence of the U.S. Embassy

Among the indigenous species of the Patagonic area we find the

Int. Seeber Square

Galileo Galilei Planetarium

This building has a theater that sits 360 people, it is properly equipped and, on its vaulted ceiling, images of the cosmos are projected. It also serves as location for scientific events and shows. A valuable metallic meteorite is exhibited on the entrance esplanade. It fell on the province of Chaco in 1965. The Planetarium is located on the corner of Sarmiento avenue and B. Roldán street.

Opening time: *Monday through Sunday, 10 AM to 6 PM.*
Guided Tours:
Saturdays and Sundays at 3 PM, 4:30 PM and 6 PM. Admission: $ 5 for adults and $ 3 for children.

Tennis Club

Av. Figueroa Alcorta

Av. Libertador

Av. Sarmiento

Monument to Sarmiento

Designed by famous French sculptor Auguste Rodin, the monument has been erected right where the house of Rosas used to stand, which is curious since he was President Sarmiento's bitterest enemy.

Zoo Garden

(see p. 79)

Monument to the Spaniard

It is a complex sculptural work finally carved in marble. It is 25 meters high and it was erected by the city as a way to honor Spanish residents.

Italy Park, Botanical Garden, Zoo and Rural exhibition center

Traveling by subway from the downtown area on line D, we stop at the Plaza Italia Metro Station. On the main route of this walk, the equestrian statue of Garibaldi stands out. On the right, we find the access to the Botanical Garden (see this page). Facing it, across Las Heras Avenue, is the main entrance to the Zoo (see p. 79) and on the opposite side of Sarmiento Avenue, there is a big exhibition center. Among the most important exhibitions thas take place there are the Buenos Aires Book Fair, ARTEBA, an important fair of art galleries, and the rural exhibition, an extremely interesting agricultural and livestock exhibition. Sarmiento Avenue ends right in the middle of Italy Park and if we walk 656 yards, we will bump into the Spaniards Monument and beyond it, the Palermo Forest.

Excursion Office, British style brick architecture. It is located in the stroll main access.

The Botanical Garden

Designed by the famous landscape designer Carlos Thays, it was inaugurated in 1902. The main entrance is at the corner of Santa Fe and Las Heras. From there on, you may walk through the main landscape route to the large greenhouse, a building that received an award in the International Exhibition of Paris. Beside it, lies a brick building, now the Excursion Office (dirección de paseos). Several sculptures decorate this area and among them, stands out Ondina del Plata by the sculptur Lucio Correa Morales. Open Tuesday to Sundays at 10 a.m.

Greenhouse.

Av. Las Heras

Gutierrez

Rep. Arabe Siria

Cabello

Latinur

Rep. de la India

Av. Cerviño

J. F. Segui

Av. Libertador

Monument to the Spaniards

Monument to Domingo F. Sarmiento

Palermo area

Zoo

Plaza Italia.
Garibaldi
Monument.

Rural Exhibition Center

Exhibition area, where the
Book Fair and ArteBA
take place.

Av. Santa Fe

Av. Sarmiento

Av. Colombia

Av. Cerviño

Juan Manuel de
Rosas Monument

The United
States Embassy

View of
Evita's Museum.

Evita Museum

This neo colonial palace houses a museum that in an entertaining and didactic way tells the life and work of Eva Perón, one of the most important and influential women of the 20th century. There are dress collections, works of art, and a complete documentation archive. The libarary and archive files of the Eva Perón Institute that operates there, are also available for consultation. In the museum's patio there is a cozy bar and restaurant.

Opening Hours: *Tuesdays to Fridays from 2 p.m. to 7:30 p.m.*
Lafinur 2988 – Teléfono: 5411-4807/9433

Zoo - Jardín Zoológico

(Open Tuesdays to Sundays and Holidays from 10 a.m. to 6 p.m.). The main entrance is at the Las Heras an Sarmiento Arcade. Upon arrival we encounter a panoramic view of the Darwin Lake, set in a romantic landscape of the 19th century. The ruins we notice on the isle of this lake, are made of authentic Byzantine marble, brought from Trieste in 1910. The Elephant Palace is a Beautiful Indian fantasy. japanese pagodas and Roman shrines complete a didactic imaginary stroll. There is a wide variety of species, as well as an aquarium and Snake Exhibit.

The area layout was designed by Carlos Thays and it was built in 1912.

If we move forward through Libertador Avenue, leaving behind the Decorative Art Museum; once we've crossed the avenue, we will arrive at an ancient grove area, among which we find grand residences and aristocratic palaces, many of them Embassies, such as the Embassy of Spain, Belgium, and Portugal.

Turning on Mariscal Castilla street, and just one block further, we will see the Grand Bourg House: a reproduction of the place where General San Martín lived his last years (see p. 83).

Directly across the street we can see the house that belonged to Victoria Ocampo, an internationally well-known intellectual that acted as patron. Figures such as Stravinsky and Tagore stayed at her house.

Through a pleasant walk of densely tree-lined curved streets, we arrive at Figueroa Alcorta Avenue at the intersection of San Martín de Tours street, where the Latin American Art Museum is located. (MALBA) (see page 84).

One block further, crossing Salguero Avenue, there is a giant Shopping Center (Paseo Alcorta), where we will find an inexpensive food terrace and amusement areas.

Walking on through Figueroa Alcorta towards the north, we find the entrance to the Japanese Garden, a peaceful oriental oasis. It is worth mentioning there is a big lake full of fishes and ducks, set among footbridges and a Japanese pavilion. Together it all forms a wonderfull landscape. There is a tea-house and an active Japanese Cultural Center.

Facing the Japanese Park, on the other side of Casares Avenue, is the Plaza Alemania (German Park). In the center of the park, there's a monument of severe lines, a creation of the sculptor Gabredón, made in 1914. It was all donated to the Argentine Republic by the German community.

Towards the south, at number 2373, we will find the José Hernández Argentine Crafts Museum (see page 82).

Vista de la Avenida Libertador hacia el Monumento de los Españoles.

Little Palermo in 3 dimensions

Reproduction of the Grand Bourg House (France).
General San Martín lived there during his last years.

Alcorta Palace. On the corner of San Martín de Tours and Figueroa Alcorta stands the Renault Museum, an excellent bar and restaurant.

Paseo Alcorta: Shopping Center, entertainment area, and food court.

O. de Ocam

Rocha

San Martín de Tours

Salguero

Av. Figueroa Alcorta

Cavila

Salguero

Av. casares

Scalabrini. Orriz

Alemania Square

Av. Libertador

82

Little Palermo

Latin American Art Museum
(MALBA)
(see p. 84)

General San Martín Monument

Victoria Ocampo's House.

Av. Figueroa Alcorta

Costa

M. Castilla

Coronel Díaz

O. de Ocampo

Av. Libertador

San Martín de Tours Church

MAMAN Art Gallery.
v. del Libertador 2475.

Under a dense green cloak, some luxurious houses can be seen. This area was designed by the landscape architect, Carlos Thays. This urban development was built in 1912, many of the palaces are now embassies. It's the most exclusive area of the city.

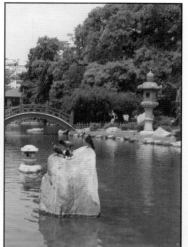

"Jose Hernández" Argentine Craft Museum

It houses a wide collection of Creole Silverware from the 19th century and there is also an exhibition of crafts from the provinces. The library is focused on folklore and can be consulted.

Opening hours: Tuesdays to Fridays from 2 p.m. to 7 p.m. Saturdays and Sundays from 3 p.m. to 7 p.m.
Avda. del Libertador 2376.

Japanese Garden: View of the lake full of fishes and ducks. The bridges and footbridges complete the oriental landscape.

MALBA Museum in 3 dimensions

Latin American Art Museum Constantini Collection.
Av. Figueroa Alcorta 3415.
Tel.: 4808-6500/98/99

In a modern building lies the recently inaugurated Latin American Art Museum of Buenos Aires. It houses the Constantini Collection, one of the few private cultural enterprises; absolutely remarkable. Works by the main Latin American painters and sculptors can be seen in its permanent exhibition room. From Botero to Frida Kahlo, and also the Argentines Antonio Berni and Xul Solar, who are very well represented in this collection.

The museum also offers a great cultural activity through films, videos, documentaries and conferences. For this purpose, it houses a spacious auditorium and a fully-equipped library.

In the ground floor hall, there's a cozy bar with a nice view and good food. Opposite to it, there is a complete bookstore that also sells works of art made by local artists at affordable prices.

Facade on Figueroa Alcorta Avenue.

Escalators take visitors to the permanent exhibition rooms on the first and second floor.

Temporary Exhibition Hall

Permanent Collection Room

Bar & Restaurant

Reception Hall & Information Point

View of the Exhibition Rooms on the second floor

Av. Figueroa Alcorta

malba | Coleccion Costantini

Access.

Bookstore.

Little Palermo

"Manifestación"
(Demostration)
Antonio Berni, Oil,
1934.

"Composición simétrica
universal"
(Universal Symmetric
Composition)
J. Torres García, Oil,
1931.

**Water
Patio**

"Los Premios" (The
Awards)
Ernesto Deira, Oil and
enamel, 1963.

**Sculptures
Terrace.**

"Composición",
Carmelo Arden Quin,
óleo y madera, 1945.

San Martín de Tours

Untitled
León Ferrari,
Steel wire, 1984.

"La Canción del Pueblo" (The People's
Song) Emilio Pettoruti, Oil, 1927.

Library.

"Los cuatro", Xul Solar, acuarela, 1921.

View of the spacious Access Hall with escalators.

**Foyer, auditori-
um and tempo-
rary exhibitions**

"Autorretrato con mono y loro"
(Self-portrait with Monkey and
Parrot) Frida Kahlo, Oil, 1942.

Tarsila do amaral
Ábaporu, Oil, 1928.

If we go back downtown along Callao avenue, we will find a large residential area. A row of buildings with luxurious apartments stands on both sides of the avenue up to the spot where it reaches Santa Fe avenue. There we find a commercial area with movie theaters, bars, bookstores and restaurants that, together with Corrientes avenue, makes up the right location for the busiest nightlife in the city. On Saturdays night, this area is very attractive and buzzing with activity.

If we keep on moving towards downtown on Callao avenue, we will reach Rodriguez Peña Square and, on the background, we will see Pizurno Palace, current seat of the Ministry of Education. If we turn right on Córdoba avenue and walk on block in the same direction, we will get to Aguas Corrientes Palace, a clay building that has been richly decorated. Some steps further, we will find Houssay Square, which is bounded by the Economics College Building and the Medicine College Building and Hospital, which make up the biggest construction in the city. The small church in the middle of the square used to be the chapel of the old Learning Hospital, which was located on those premises. If we walk back to Callao avenue and we keep moving along it, we will get to Corrientes avenue.

Barrio Norte in 3 dimensions

The Medicine College Building covers the whole block and it is the biggest construction in the city. It was built in the 1930s.

Clinicas Hospital

Housay Square

Facultad de Ciencias Economicas

Tímpano de la Facultad de Ciencias Económicas sobre la Av. Córdoba.

Clásica y moderna es un bar-restaurante-librería, muy conocido.

La iglesia del Carmen: Su amplio atrio contrasta con el templo de pequeñas dimensiones.

Iglesia y Colegio del Salvador. Construida por la orden de los Jesuitas, se inaugura en 1876, la iglesia es de tres naves y está ricamente decorada con pinturas en Trompe o'eil. El colegio ocupa el resto de la manzana y es uno de los colegios católicos más tradicionales de la ciudad.

Algunas de las más bellas cúpulas asoman a la Av. Callao, la de la foto está en Callão y Lavalle.

Aguas Corrientes Palace: This gaudy building entirely decorated with English ceramic houses 12 water reservoirs, each of which can hold 70 million liters of water. Its strong outside walls are 1.80 meters thick. This palace, built in 1887, has been mentioned by Jorge Luis Borges in some of his stories, poems and essays.

Ex Movie Theater Gran Splendid, reciclaed in a greit bookstore.

Movie theaters, restaurants and bookstores area

School Normal Nº1

Riobamba

Av. Callao

Av. Santa Fe

Marcelo T. de Alvear

Paraguay

Av. Cordoba

Rodriguez Peña

Notorius: CD's, bar, restaurant, shous. Callao 966, Tel.: 4815-8473.

Rodríguez Peña Square

Several Petit Hotels are still standing in this area of the city.

Pizurno Palace: it is the current seat of the Ministry of Education. It was designed in an elegant and harmonious French style and its walls bear an original bossage.

Corrientes Avenue

Obelisk in 3 dimensions

It was built in the 1930s by architect Prebich. It stands there to commemorate the place where the Argentinian flag was hoisted for the first time. The Church of St Nicholas used to be located on these plot of land and it was later moved to Santa Fe avenue, between Talcahuano and Uruguay streets.

Subway line "B". Station Carlos Pellegrini.

Subway line "C". Station Diagonal Norte.

Subway line "D". Station 9 de julio.

Stairwat into the Obelisk.

Comertial Pasagge

Diagonal Norte

Carlos Pellegrini

Av. 9 de Julio

Cerrito

Carlos Pellegrini

De la Republica Square.

Av. Corrientes

Av. 9 de Julio

Access to the Subway

Cerrito

Comertial Pasagge

Corrientes Avenue

Corrientes avenue is the axis of cultural life in the city of Buenos Aires. There are corners and addresses on it that make up the essence of tango, such as Corrientes 348 or the corner of Corrientes and Esmeralda street. A narrower Corrientes was, until the 1930s, the street where all tango celebrities used to gather. After the middle-1930s, it was widened and it became an avenue. It was only then that theaters and cinemas started to come up along it and it turned into the Argentinian Broadway. Undoubtedly, walking along Corrientes avenue in the evening is a must. A view of this avenue with the Obelisk on the background makes the typical postcard of Buenos Aires.

By the end of the 1950s, San Martín Theater and Cultural Center were built on Corrientes, which added another point of interest to the avenue. Theaters, cinemas, bars and libraries give it a bohemian and intellectual atmosphere. On next page, you will find a guide to the points of interest on Corrientes avenue.

Corrientes Avenue in 3 dimensions

De las Naciones Hotel

La Ideal Bar, Tango

Blanca Podesta Theater

Domingo F. Sarmiento's home

Opera Theater

Metropolitan Theater

Gran Rex Theater

Panamericano Hotel

El Nacional Theater

Obelisk

Broadway Theater

Tribunales

Lola Membrives Theater

Lorca Cinema

Suipacha

Av. Corrientes

Sarmiento

Av. 9 de Julio

Av. Corrientes

C. Pellegrini

Av. 9 de Julio

Cerrito

Tucumán

Libertad

Lavalle

Uruguay

Tucumán

La Academia: a traditional bar on the corner of Callao and Corrientes avenues.

El Gato Negro: shop that specializes in coffee, spices and aromatic herbs. Corrientes 1669.

Losada, bookstore, theater, bar.

Banchero: typical pizza house in Buenos Aires.

92

La Paz: traditional bar and restaurant that serves as meeting point for artists and intellectuals, on the corner of Corrientes avenue and Montevideo street.

Gandhi: it houses a bar, a bookstore, a record store and an auditorium. It serves as meeting point for artists and intellectuals and it is one of the most interesting spots on Corrientes1747.

La Plaza: entertainment complex with theaters, bars, record stores and bookstores in a natural ambience. An excellent spot on Corrientes 1660.

Cooperation Cultural Center
It is a modern art and cultural center. It houses a large auditorium. and an exhibition room. Many teaching activities also take place.

La Giralda Bar

San Martín Theater (see p. 94).

Bar La Paz

La Plaza. *Theaters, bar and restaurants*

Sarmiento

Ramos Bar

La Academia. *Bar.*

Gandi bookstore

Rodriguez Peña

Montevideo

Lavalle

La Giralda: inexpensive and traditional bar the specialty of which is hot chocolate and fritter. Corrientes 1453.

Alvear Theater

Astral Theater

Cine Los Angeles. kids movies.

Av. Callao

Av. Corrientes

Riobamba

San Martín Theater and Cultural Center in 3 dimensiones

In 1960, the most modern and functional building of its time was opened in Buenos Aires. The huge complex had been designed by architect Mario Roberto Alvarez for the purpose of housing theaters, auditoriums, small movie projection rooms, etc.

The complex covers 29,350 square meters and both wings look clean and tidy at first sight, with enormous glass surfaces and powerful pillars that may be seen in the entrance hall.

It houses three theaters. The biggest one is called Martin Coronado and it can sit up to 1700 people. It is one of the newest and best-equipped halls in the city and its stage has witnessed the presence of the best local and international actors.

The Casacuberta theater is two stories below it, in the underground level, and it sits 560 people. It was designed as an amphitheater and it serves to put on plays that need more intimacy.

Across from the Casacuberta theater, in a spacious hall, you will find a huge mural painting 35 meters long and 11 meters high by Spanish artist Luis Seoane. It depicts theater pioneers in Argentina. On the 10th floor you will find

Leopoldo Lugones hall, a small movie theater where artistic movies are usually projected.

The huge entrance hall usually serves as stage for free, world-class shows in the afternoon and evening.

The San martin theater has been joined to the San martin Cultural Center on Sarmiento avenue through a passage on the ground floor, where a photographs exhibition gallery directed by prestigious photographer Sara Facio is located.

In the entrance area of this gallery you will find a sculpture by Sesostris Vitullo called Martín Fierro.

The San Martin Cultural Center houses many exhibition rooms, a hall for experimental theater, an auditorium and an enormous convention hall. In the same building you will find the Tourism Department of the City of Buenos Aires, the Municipal Radio Station and a Conservatory of Music.

Municipal Radio Station.

Enrique Muiño Hall.

Convention halls A and B.

Sarmiento

Sculptures Square.

Paraná

Experimental theater hall.

"The Equilibrists", bronze sculpture by Curatella Manes. You will find it in the sculpture patio on the corner of Sarmiento and Paraná streets.

The main theater companies in the world have visited the stages of the different halls in San Martin theater.

Teatro San Martín

San Martín Cultural Center

View of the huge central hall on the ground floor.

San Martín Theatre

Facade of San Martin theater.

Leopoldo Lugones hall, movie theater.

Offices.

Av. Corrientes

Entrance Hall.

Subway, Line B.

Workshops.

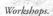

Martín Coronado Theater hall.

Casacuberta theater hall.

Jennifer Muller, dancer.

Oscar Araiz, choreographer

Alfredo Alcón, Actor

Jorge Lavelli, director

Lavalle Square

In 1840, Mariano Miró and Felisa Dorrego bought the lands where part of the square is located today and they built a huge mansion called Miró Palace, in the gardens of which they planted a collection of trees, many of which still survive.

The mansion was demolished in 1937 in order to add those lands to the square, which thus covered the three blocks it still covers today. We suggest that you take a slow walk around the square and take your time to watch the sculptures and trees closely (see next page).

Among the buildings whose facade looks upon the square, we should mention the Federal Courthouse, Roca School, the Colon Theater, Cervantes Theater and the Sinagogue of the Israeli Congregation in Argentina, where the square meets Tucumán street. In the middle of the square you will find a column with the statue of Juan Lavalle on top of it. The square has been named after him and he was a military man educated in San Martin's army. His life was pretty violent and he was the worst enemy of Dorrego's (governor of the province of Buenos Aires), a man he later had executed by shooting. Dorrego happened to be one of Felisa Dorrego's predecessors.

Lavalle Square in 3 dimensions

Cervantes Theater

Spanish actress María Guerrero had it built as a tribute to the city of Buenos Aires. It was opened in 1921 and, in 1961, its stage was renovated and a new wing that actually serves as workshop was added. Currently, it is the most important public theater in terms of dramatic plays. On the corner of Córdoba avenue and Libertad street, you will find the entrance door to the National Museum of Theater, where collections and documents on Argentinian theater's history are exhibited.

Opening time: Monday through Friday, 1 PM to 6:30 PM.

Cervantes Theater in 3 dimensions

Libertad

Av. Córdoba

Agatis Robusta: Gigantic tree, 120 years old.

Massüe Mirador: It is one of the few examples of Art Nouveau architecture in the city.

President Roca School: *Greek-style building which has a magnificent facade with Ionic columns.*

Colón Theater *(see p. 100-101).*

Ficus macrophyllia: *A tree whose trunk is over 80 meters in diameter.*

Carlos Pellegrini

Av. 9 de Julio

Cerrito

Libertad

Av. Córdoba

Sinagogue of the Israeli Congregation in Argentina: *Its looks upon Libertad street. The building dates from 1932 and it is one of the main synagogues in the city.*

María Guerrero Garden

Lavalle Square

Obelisk
(see p. 90)

Edelweiss Restaurant: it is the traditional place to go for dinner after a show in the Colon Theater.

Av. Corrientes

Diagonal Norte

Artists Tenement House: This building is located at Libertad 543. It dates from 1907 and it has served as the house for many artists' workshops since 1966.

Second-hand books market.

Monumento to victims of AMIA

Lavalle

Tucumán

Statue of Juan Lavalle.

Federal Courthouse: *It is the seat of the judicial body. The project was designed by architect Norberto Maillard and construction began in 1889 but it only finished in 1942, after many disputes had taken place. It is an eclectic building and, undoubtedly, its monumental sense of esthetics is pretty questionable.*

Talcahuano

Viamonte

Trajano Emperor

Jujuy's Ceibo Tree: Historic tree that was planted in 1878.

99

Colón Theater in 3 dimensions

Facade of Colon Theater on Libertad street.

The first building for the Colon Theater was located on Av de Mayo, where the National Bank stands today. By the end of the 19th Century, Buenos Aires had become a wealthy city and the theater was not as luxurious as the new generations wanted it to be, so the project for a new Colon Theater was designed. The original plans were drawn by Italian architect Francisco Tamburini and submitted for approval in 1829. The theater was to be located in front of Lavalle Square. After a series of never-ending difficulties, architect Julio Dormal finally finished it in 1908. The main theater has a seating capacity of 2,500 and it may accommodate up to 3,500 people if standing tickets are sold. The main entrance door to the orchestra floor and boxes is on Libertad street and the higher seating rows in the theater may be entered though the entrance doors on Toscanini and Tucumán streets.

The main hall is enormous and it is entirely covered in stucco that has been molded by Italian artisans. There is a combination of styles that may be appreciated by seeing the Ionic and Corinthian capitals. On the ceiling, there is a French stained-glass piece.

The main staircase leading to the theater itself is made up of a combination of Carrara marbles from Verona and Portugal. The banister's tops are craved by a famous sculptor called

Chapasco. In this hall you will find a small museum of history of the Colon Theater and a museum of old and valuable musical instruments. There is also a public library that has books on music and opera. If you go up any of the lateral stairs, you will get to the hall of Busts, a long wide corridor where you will find the faces of the most famous musicians of all times on the lintels. One of the lateral walks will take you to the Golden Hall, an exquisitely decorated room with gilded details and French furniture, chandeliers and vases.

The main theater has an Italian-style horseshoe design, there are three stories with boxes on balconies, then a gallery for women, an upper gallery, another gallery above it and finally a paradise or top gallery. The theater is 33 meters in diameter and 28 meters high. The dome's ceiling was painted by famous artist Raúl Soldi. The main chandelier is a unique piece with more than 600 light bulbs. It weighs 2,500 kilos and a maximum of 20 people can stand inside of it to create sound effects during the show.

White hall.

Main Theater.

Stage.

Performer's entrance door.

Costume design workshop.

Zapatería.

Peluquería.

Oficina técnica.

View of the canopy built on the entrance door after the opening.

Taller de escenografía.

Theater with dome's ceiling painted by Raúl Soldi and main chandelier with over 600 light bulbs.

Main Hall.

Golden Hall.

View of the upper galleries as seen from the entrance hall.

Entrance for visitors.

Guided tours: Monday through Friday: 9 AM, 10 AM, 11 AM, 12 AM, 1 PM, 2 PM, 3 PM and 4 PM. Saturdays: : 9 AM, 10 AM, 11 AM and 12 AM. Admission: $ 5. Toscanini street 1180. Information: 4382-6632.

Storege Rooms.

Hall of Busts.

Dance hall

workshop

Balconies with caryatids on the facade upon Libertad street.

Machinery and Carpenter's workshop

Facade on Toscanini street.

Sculpture workshop

Stage designers workshop on the third underground level.

Colon Theater: its Workshops and Companies

The theater's workshops are located in the underground levels. It is one of the few opera houses in the world in which most of the articles needed for the show may be produced. It has a stage designers workshop, a hairdresser's, a shoemaking workshop, a costume design workshop, a carpenter's workshop, etc.

Quite an army of people work in these underground levels, which stretch below Viamonte street and 9 de Julio avenue.

The Colon Theater has its own art companies: a Philharmonic Orchestra, a Choir and a Ballet Company. There are over one hundred company members in all.

The main opera and ballet starts in the world have set foot on the theater's stage, among them we can mention: Lili Pons, Enrique Caruso, María Callas and Luciano Pavarotti (the most famous opera singers in this century) as well as Rudolf Nureyev and Nijinsky (the main ballet dancers). Julio Boca, Maximiliano Herrera and Paloma Herrera, the most important ballet dancers from Argentina, were educated in the Colon Theater's school. Among musicians and conductors, we should mention the performance of Richard Strauss in 1920, as well as the concerts given by Igor Stravinsky and the unforgettable shows of Pablo Casals and Manuel de Falla. Arturo Toscanini conducted the theater's orchestra in many opportunities and it is in his honor that one of the lateral streets of the theater has been called Toscanini.

Sculpture storage room on the third underground level.

The list of famous performers is never-ending, but we could also mention the Vienna Boys' Choir, Alfredo Kraus, José Carreras, Plácido Domingo, Herbert Von Karajian, Maurice Bejart, Margot Fontaine, Maia Plissetskaya, etc.

Scene of Les Sylphides.

Marcia Haydee and the Stuttgart Ballet.

Astor Piazzolla: he gave his consecrating concert in the theater.

Richard Strauss conducted in the Colon Theater during his two visits to Buenos Aires.

Beniamino Gigli performed in the theater many seasons.

Mascagni conducted his Cavalleria rusticana in 1911.

The Great Domes

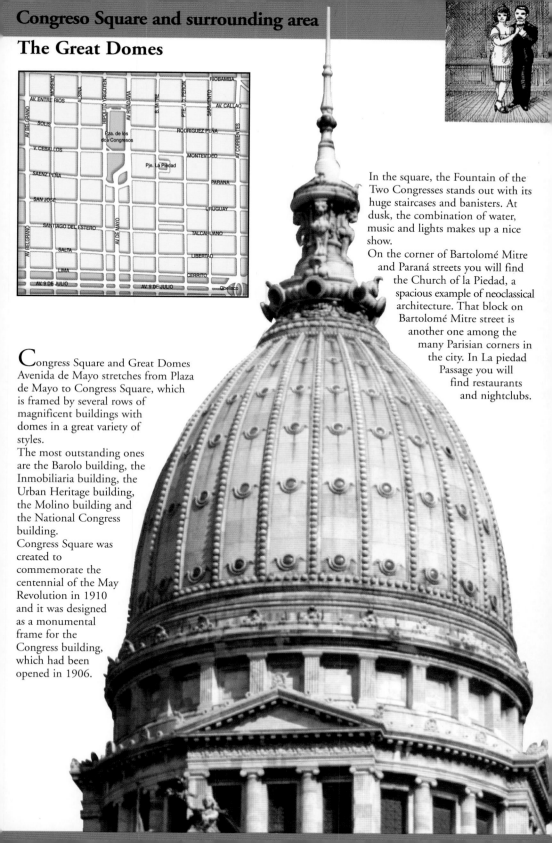

In the square, the Fountain of the Two Congresses stands out with its huge staircases and banisters. At dusk, the combination of water, music and lights makes up a nice show.

On the corner of Bartolomé Mitre and Paraná streets you will find the Church of la Piedad, a spacious example of neoclassical architecture. That block on Bartolomé Mitre street is another one among the many Parisian corners in the city. In La piedad Passage you will find restaurants and nightclubs.

Congress Square and Great Domes Avenida de Mayo stretches from Plaza de Mayo to Congress Square, which is framed by several rows of magnificent buildings with domes in a great variety of styles.

The most outstanding ones are the Barolo building, the Inmobiliaria building, the Urban Heritage building, the Molino building and the National Congress building.

Congress Square was created to commemorate the centennial of the May Revolution in 1910 and it was designed as a monumental frame for the Congress building, which had been opened in 1906.

Congreso Square in 3 dimensions

The area is full of cafés and bars with tables on the sidewalk, and there are also some theaters and nightclubs. The most important theater among them is Avenida Theater, a traditional house where zarzuelas (Spanish form of light opera) are usually performed. A group of excellent Spanish restaurants surrounds the theater. Across the street from the square, on Rivadavia street, you will see Liceo Theater, a traditional old little theater.

The Avila Bar on Av de Mayo 1300 and Agua y Fuego on Rivadavia 1400 are nice places to have dinner in and enjoy Flamenco shows at the same time.

Photos: Otilio Moralejo.

Former Magestic hotel, square dome. (see p. 108).

Dome of the building next to the National Senate, located in Alsina street and Entre Rios avenue.

Estatue to the Thinking man by Auguste Rodin

Pinacle of the dome of La Inmobiliaria building.(see p. 108).

Meson Español. Restaurant El Imparcial spanish food. Salta 97

Restaurant El Globo spanish food. Salta 98

Avenida Theater

Restaurant Hispano Espanish food. Salta 26

Castelar Hotel

Dome of Urban Heritage Building, located in Rivadavia av. and Parana street

LA CUEVA bookstore Av. de Mayo 1119.

San José

Santiago del Estero

Hipolito Yrigoyen

Salta

Lima

Libertad

Av. de Mayo

Rivadavia

Cerrito

Av. 9 de Julio

Avila. Restaurant
Spanish food.
Av. de Mayo 1384

Liceo Theater Av. Entre Ríos

Solís

Virrey Cevallos

Hipólito Yrigoyen

Av. Rivadavia

Av. Callao

Rodríguez Peña

Montevideo

nz. Peña

Paraná

Rivadavia

Uruguay

Chile Hotel

36 billares bar

cahuano

Main body of
the Monument
to the two
Congresses

Monumental lighthouse pinnacle in Barolo
Building (see p. 107)

Art-noveau dome. Former Café del
Molino building.

Ornamental pinacle of
National Congress' dome
(see p. 110)

Photo: Otilio Moralejo.

105

Barolo Building:

The successive curve and straight lines of balconies and cornices convey a dramatic style to the tower.
Metallic structure where the revolving lighthouse is placed.

It dates from 1922 and it was designed by Italian architect Mario Palanti. For a period, it was the highest building in Buenos Aires. A rare example of expressionist architecture, it has a monumental appearance and a spacious gallery that reaches Hipólito Irigoyen street. Even though this gallery is somehow deteriorated, it is still faithful to its original appearance. If you take a close look at the building, you will find some hidden esoteric details included by architect Palanti, such as the gargoyles, the dragons, the circles and the balustrades that may be seen in the main vault.
The number and measures of these elements have been taken from figures and keys provided by Dante in The Divine Comedy.

Metallic structure where the revolving lighthouse is placed.

Photo: Otilio Moralejo.

The perspective on Av. de Mayo makes Barolo building look as one of the most outstanding buildings in the city.

Access to offices.

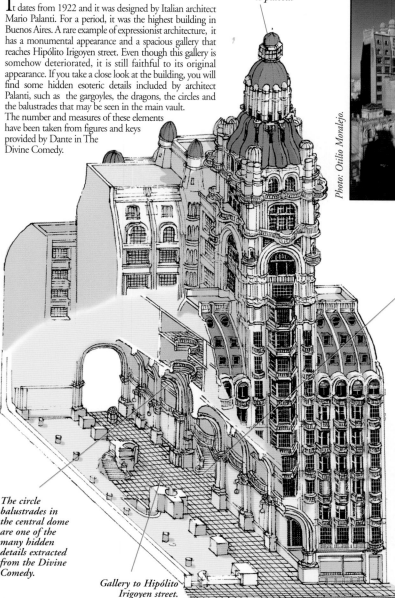

Dome of the gallery where the access to stairs and lifts is located.

The circle balustrades in the central dome are one of the many hidden details extracted from the Divine Comedy.

Gallery to Hipólito Irigoyen street.

La Inmobiliaria Building

The work of Luis Broggi, inaugurated on 25 May 1910, ordered by the insurance company La Inmobiliaria .It takes up the whole length of the street. Two high towers crowned by domes indicate the corners.

Balcony on the second floor imitating a renacentist loggia.

Embossed metal pinacle completing the corner domes.

Pte. Luis Sáenz Peña

San José

Av. de Mayo

Former Crítica Newspaper

Built by architect Kalnay. It is a strange example of art-deco architecture and expressionist elements.

Av. de Mayo

Former Majestic Hotel

It serves as headquarters for a government office nowadays but it used to be one of the main hotels in the city. Its robust frame has a square dome on top of it. This is the place where Nijinsky resided during his stay in Buenos Aires.

Chile Hotel

A solid frame with art-noveau decoration. The corner balcony was completed by a onion-shaped dome conveying an oriental-style to its lines. It is located in 1400 Av. de Mayo.

Santiago del Estero

Avenida Theater

It was recently restored after a fire. It is one of the most important and traditional theaters for light opera.

Sala en forma de herradura ubicada en diagonal con respecto a la Av. de Mayo.

Facade of Avenida Theater.

Neoclassical-style pinacle of La Piedad church's bell tower.

Av. de Mayo

De la Piedad Church

1524 Bartolomé Mitre.
This church was designed in a typical neoclassical style with a huge central nave and a high dome. The church is richly decorated on the inside and it has icons that date from the 18th Century.

Neoclassical-style pinacle of La Piedad church's bell tower.

Paraná

Bmé. Mitre

El Tumi: Restaurant, Peruan food

De la Piedad Passage

Charming spot in the city built as a condominium at the beginning of this Century. It has gone through terrible deterioration and mutilations over the years, but its charm is still intact. The outside street has a nice Parisian touch and the narrow inside passages remind us of some places in Rome.

National Congress in 3 dimensions

Foto: Otilia Moralejo.

monumentality and Greek austerity. The huge central dome of the National Congress building is meant to remind us of its sister in Washington. The building bears some perfectly carved caryatids, quadrigas and capitals you should not miss. Inside of it, there is a series of beautiful halls and a library with a wide range of valuable and out of print books. It houses the two chambers that make up Argentina's legislative body: the Chamber

Under a law enacted in 1889, the National Congress was moved to the lands of an old sawmill on the block bound by Callao street, Hipólito Irigoyen street, Pozos street and Rivadavia avenue.

In 1896, once Av de Mayo had been finished, the government opened an international bidding for the building's construction works. As a result of this process, construction of the building was left in the hands of architect Victor Meano, who had been working in the country for a while and helping architect Tamburini in the Colon Theater project and other buildings.

The National Congress is a monumental building in a classic Greek-Latin style. It may be viewed properly from Av de Mayo, which makes up an axis with the Executive Office Building or Pink House on one end and the

Hipólito Yrigoyen

National Congress, which houses the legislative body, on the other one. The National Congress was opened in 1906 and the buildings that surround it were finished in 1910, for the Independence Centennial celebrations.

Its decoration is made up of a combination of marble and granite, which gathers both Roman

of Representatives covers the back central area of the building and its semicircular shape may be seen from Pozos street, where as the Chamber of Senators is located in the left wing of the building and it is quite smaller. Undoubtedly, the most magnificent spot in the building is the Blue Hall, which lies under the big

View of the Congress as seen from Av de Mayo.

Chamber of Representantes.

Hall of the Lost Paces.

Chamber of Senators.

Blue hall.

Pink hall.

Reading Hall for the Chamber of Senators.

Av. Callao

Big Hall

Library

Caryatids at the National Congress' side doors.

dome (approx. 60 meters high). The ceiling bears some beautiful marble cravings, some allegoric statues and a 2-ton chandelier made up of bronze and Baccarat crystal.

Greek-Roman style decoration.

place where historic events of national importance occured, such as the ratification of the Constitution in 1853 by Urquiza and the conclusion of San José de Flores Agreement on November 11, 1859.

Later on, many of those country houses were divided in smaller plots of land of 8.66 meters' wide. Family houses were built and turned the town into an urban area.

By the end of the 18th Century, Juan Diego Flores owned a plot of land that extended from the current Flores Cementry to Alvarez Jonte avenue, including the area where the commercial part of the neighborhood is now located. After his death in 1801, his adopted child Ramón Francisco Flores and the family's attorney Antonio Millán, planned a new town to both sides of the Camino Real "Royal Road" (now known as Rivadavia avenue) and sold the pieces of land. They also granted a block for the construction of a church, another one for a square and a third one for the public slaughterhouses. The names of the towns used to be related to the owner of the land and that is the reason why Flores family's name identified the place as such. A new ecclesiastical jurisdiction was created on May 31, 1806: San José de Flores Parish. It gave its name to this new town, which then became a provincial district and, lastly, a neighborhood of the City of Buenos Aires. As time went by, San José de Flores became a resting place for rich people who lived in the city center. The country houses and mansions that were built in the area gave rise to a splendorous and luxurious era. Important characters used to own a piece of property in Flores. It was the perfect scenery for giving magnificent parties, but it was also the

Basilica of San José de Flores. This neoclassical church was erected in 1883 and its inner part is richly decorated.

Flores in 3 dimensions

Mural by Juan Carlos Castagnino. Photograph: Pablo Reales.

Murals in Galería San José de Flores:

Rivadavia avenue 6836

It was opened on November 10, 1956 by José R. Angelelli and it became the most exclusive shopping place of the neighborhood. Its elegant and well-furnished shops are displayed in a T-shaped area. It also has an entrance door on Membrillar street and another one on Ramón L. Falcón street. It is worth a visit because it turns out to be a pleasant trip and due to the magnificent murals in the central dome by Juan Carlos Castagnino (1908-1972), Enrique Policastro (1898-1971) and Demetrio Urruchúa (1902-1978), exponents of the social realism in Argentina.

Inner part of San José de Flores church. The outstanding decorative painting can be seen in this photograph.

School and Museum Gral. Urquiza.

School Number 2 "Florencio Varela". Typical bricked-style building.

Flores Neighborhood

Pueyrredón
Square

School Fernando Fader,
ex Palace Las Lilas

Culpina

Av. Rivadavia

Pje. La Porteña

Varela

Yerbal

Bolivia

Artigas

Estación San
José de Flores

Vías del Ferrocarril Sarmiento

Fray Cayetano Rodriguez

Caracas

Pje. Marcoartú

View of the sidewalk where the
back of Banco Nación's
building is located. To both
sides of the Basilica, you can
walk along narrow lanes that
are unique.

Dense vegetation of
the streets
sorrounding
the square.

Rivadavia avenue,
which used to be
called Camino Real
del Oeste (West
Royal Road), is the
longest avenue in
the world.

Marcó del Pont
Mansion. Artigas
street 20. It was
erected in 1871. It has
been restored and is
now the seat of a
Cultural Center.

Northof Palermo, if you walk along Cabildo or Luis María Campos avenues, you will reach Belgrano neighborhood.

Subway line "D" also reaches Belgrano's commercial area, above Juramento station.

Near middle 19th Century, Belgrano was a settlement apart from the City of Buenos Aires; in 1880, it became the seat of the National Government due to political circumstances. It was in said year that Belgrano was made a city on its own, but in the 1890s it had already become part of the capital city.

The historic area surrounds General Manuel Belgrano square, where you may find a crafts market on Saturdays and Sundays. Across from the square, on the corner of Juramento avenue and Vuelta de Obligado street, you will find the Museum of Sapnish Art "Enrique Larreta". The neocolonial building was erected in 1916 and it was home to writer Enrique Larreta.

In front of the square, near Arcos street, you will also find "Sarmiento Museum", which was seat to the National Government in 1880. It has been open since 1938 as a museum devoted to former President Domingo Faustino Sarmiento.

Photo: Otilio Moraleja.

Belgrano Neighborhood in 3 dimensions

Photo: Otilio Moralejo.

View of the Inmaculada
Concepción Church, also known
as "La Redonda". Its dome can be
seen above the dense vegetation
that surrounds it.

*Subway station
Juramento, line D.*

> ***Sarmiento History Museum***
> *Cuba 2079.*
> ***tours:*** *thursday to Sunday from
> 15 p.m. to 19 p.m.*

Metalic gazebo located
in Barrancas de
Belgrano park.

Undoubtely, the most outstanding building that you can see from the square is the Inmaculada Concepción Church, also known as "La Redonda" (the Round Church), which was opened in 1878. The main body of this unusual church is round and it is framed by two symmetrical shelters.

Until mid 20th. Century, the area was characterized by huge houses and tree-lined streets and avenues. Nowadays, the trees have become green domes that protect walkers from the sun and make it extremely pleasant to walk along those streets in the summer.

The high rise apartment buildings that have recently been erected (most of which are higher than 30 floors), together with the old mansions provide a modern and, at the same time, traditional profile to the neighborhood.

The main commercial areas in the neighborhood are located along most of Cabildo avenue and Juramento avenue, between Cabildo and Barrancas de Belgrano.

Barrancas de Belgrano is the most important green area in the neighborhood. It is a huge park surrounded by enormous modern-style buildings. Among these buildings, you will find the "Libero Badii Museum", an old mansion devoted to the work of the Italian sculpture and painter it is named after.

The park was redesigned in 1892 by landscape designer Carlos Thays. Barrancas de Belgrano is plenty of miradors and terraces, and it also has a wonderful metalic gazebo. Among the numerous plants and trees that can be found in the park, you may see centennial magnolias. A scale reproduction of New York's Statue of Liberty stands among the trees.

If you walk five blocks from Barrancas de Belgrano, along Luis María Campos avenue, you will reach "El Solar de la Abadía" shopping mall. Both the mall and its surroundings are among the most sophisticated and exclusive areas of the city. There, we will find excellent restaurants.

*Mirador localted on
Sucre street in Barrancas
de Belgrano park. It pro-
vides an excellent view of
the surrounding area.*

Rogelio Yrurtia Museum.

Facade of the Rogelio Yrurtia Museum. O'Higgins 2390 Opened wednesday to friday from 15 to 19:30 p.m.. Saturday from 16 to 20 p.m.

Líbero Badii Museum.

"Descent". Polychrome wood carving, 17th. Century.

China Town:

If you cross Virrey Vertiz avenue and the railways through Belgrano station, you will find "China Town", which is located along Arribeños, Montañeses, Mendoza and Juramento streets. There is plenty of Chinese restaurants, grocery stores and shops selling imported goods from the East. There are also some Buddhist temples and a monastery.

Barrancas de Belgrano

Mendoza

Juramento

O'Higgins

Zavala

Echeverria

Sucre

Virrey Vertiz

Estación Belgrano C "FFCC Mitre"

Arribeños

Mendoza

Juramento

Montañeses

Museum of sapanish Art Enrique Larreta

It is a museum devoted to Spanish art. It features works that date from 13th. to 20th. Centuries, such as colorful carvings and altarpieces. The building represents the style of early 20th. Century mansions in Belgrano neighborhood. Its large Andalusian garden with Moorish fountains is unique.

Juramento 2291. Tel: 4784-4040
Admission: $1, Tuesdays free.
Opening time: Mondays, Thursdays, Fridays and weekends from 3 PM to 8 PM.
Guided tours:
Sundays at 4 PM and 6 PM.

Vista de una de las salas del museo.

Argentine Museum of Natural Sciences
Bernardino Rivadavia

The Museum is located in the Parque Centenario Area, on 400 Angel Gallardo avenue. It was opened in 1812 and it had several seats until the current building was finished in 1937 by architect Cristophersen. Its outer and inner decoration made up of sculptures and bass-relieves features animals and plants from the area. Reknown artists such as Juan del Prete have contributed to the museum's decoration. We will manage to discover these works of art if we take time and examine all the details, such as the owls (symbols of wisdom) and the spider webs on the entrance gate.

In the entrance hall, you will find huge metalic meteors that were found in Argentina. You may visit a large hall containing a collection of minerals and scale reproductions of the surface of the Earth.

To the left of the entrance hall, there is a small aquarium with exotic species and an area with a complete collection of shells.

Museum of Natural Sciences

Undoubtedly, the most interesting part of the museum is the Paleontology Hall, probably the most important of its kind in Latin America. When you visit the hall, you will see many dinosaurs that have been found in Argentina by the museum's research teams. Among them, there are Carnotaurs and Glyptodonts, prehistoric inhabitants of the area now covered by the City of Buenos Aires.

On the first floor, there is a Compared Anatomy area and a large hall of birds, where we can appreciate a wide variety of South American species, many of which are placed in dioramas that reproduce their natural habitat.

One of the wings on the first floor is full of whales' bones and other marine mammals' skeletons.

Last but not least, the arthropods hall contains several collections displayed in windows following didactic criteria.

Artropodos

View of the Paleontology Hall, dinosaurs found in Argentina on the foreground.

Address:
Angel Gallardo 490, Capital Federal.
Opening time:
*Monday through Sunday
from 2 PM to 7 PM.*
Admission: $1.
Transport:
*Bus 15, 36, 55, 65, 92, 99, 105,
112, 124, 135, 141 and 146.*
Subway Line B:
*Angel Gallardo station
(6 blocks from the museum).*
Guided tours:
*Tuesdays and Thursdays 10 AM
(English and French
requests at 4982-4494).*

On the first floor, there are dioramas displaying native species in their natural habitat. In this case, ostriches and deers in the Pampa area.

Photo: Otilio Moralejo

PASTIZAL PAMPEANO

El museo posee varios ejemplares de carnotauros, como el de la ilustración.

Glyptodont: the natural habitat of this species was the Pampa planes. Some of them have been found on excavations in the area of the City of Buenos Aires.

Cetacea and Mammals Hall, first floor.

Birds Hall.

Main entrance.

Geology and Minerology Hall.

123

El Abasto

In 1890, a foodstuffs market called Abasto was erected on Corrientes avenue. Some time later, a new neighborhood started to grow around it and it took the market's name. In 1931, construction works began for a new market building in modernist Art-decó style with big domes in reinforced concrete.

In the early 20th Century, when the first market was built, the area took a different shape thanks to the presence of carriages, laborers, hostels and canteens which gave it a marginal ambience where tango music, popular songs and people's poetry were easily spread. One of the most important tango figures that lived in the area was Carlos Gardel, the city's mythical singer. Today, a street and a subway station that carry his name remind us of his presence in the neighborhood. The area is taking new shape again now: high-rise apartment buildings, five-star hotels, night clubs and theaters are being built and the old market has become a giant shopping mall.

View of the old market in the 1930s.

Hipermarket

Shooping Abasto

Gallo

Guardia Vieja

Lavalle

Anchorena

Carlos Gardel

Agüero

Av. Corrientes

Monument to mythical singer Carlos Gardel, by sculptor Mariano Pages.

"Holiday Inn" International Hotel, world class hotel located in the heart of the neighborhood.

Detalle de la arqueria monumental.

Interior of the restored building where a giant shopping mall stands today.

The Argentine tango and its characteristics

The origins of tango music date back to the period that stretches from the 1850s to the 1880s. Tango music is deeply influenced by African-American rhythms, such as candombe and habanera, and by some European dances, such as Spanish contredanse and the so-called Andalusian tango. Those are the predecessors of Argentinian tango. In the late 19th Century, the so-called suburban tango became consolidated. At the beginning, people used to dance the tango in the suburbs and it was not until the early 20th Century that it was accepted as a decent dance in luxurious downtown dance halls. Tango music later took its strength of character and melancholy cadence from the mainly Italian and Spanish immigrants that arrived in the city at the begining of this Century. Around 1910, tango music had already spread to Europe and it was widely accepted in all the big cities in the world, whereas in Buenos Aires it still aroused suspicion, specially among members of the Catholic Church, who even condemned it. Hansen's, the Armenonville and Chanteclair were the places where this dance was first accepted and their customers quickly became fans of it. Dance parties and meetings started to spread all around the city at a fast pace and thus appeared the greatest tango composers,

Corrientes street before it became an avenue.

performers, dancers and writers in the city. At this stage, the bandoneon became the main musical instrument in Typical Orchestras, that is, tango orchestras created by Vicente Greco. In the 1920s, tango music became worldwide famous and Buenos Aires, which was enjoying good economical conditions at the time, show itself as the Queen of the River Plate. Its nightlife gained fame together with Corrientes street (which had not become an avenue yet) and it huge cabarets. This situation lead tango music to its golden period. The most important figure in tango music is Carlos Gardel, a mythical singer born in France and raised in the Abasto market neighborhood who possessed a great deal of magnetism and a privileged voice. Carlos Gardel was responsible for taking tango music to Broadway and Hollywood.

Vicente Greco

Carlos Gardel with the so-called New York Blondes: he embodies the myth of the Argentine winner who attains success in Hollywood.

The protagonists

Agustin Bardi, Julio Decaro, Celedonio Flores, Discépolo, Osvaldo Fresedo, Osvaldo Pugliese and Aníbal Troilo were the main tango composers and performers in Argentina. In the 1920-1950 period several tango schools were created: some of them supported sung tango and focused on the poetics of the lyrics, whereas others, such as that of Aníbal Troilo or Osvaldo Pugliese, supported the dance side of tango. Among great tango singers we should mention Julio Sosa, Edmundo Rivero, Roberto Goyeneche, Libertad Lamarque and Hugo del Carril. Tango lyrics writers were great poets, as is the case with Homero Manzi, Horacio Ferrer, and even Jorge Luis Borges himself, who did not miss the chance to write the lyrics of some famous tango songs.

Astor Piazzolla, a musician and disciple of Aníbal Troilo, was also the last great innovator in tango music. He placed tango music closer to contemporary music and was widely accepted and acknowledged as one of the greatest composers of these times. Nowadays, thousands of tourist arrive in Buenos Aires with a main goal: watching tango shows and learning how to dance to the beat of this fascinating music that is, as a great poet once said, "a sad feeling you can dance to".

Francisco Canaro's Tango Orchestra

Homero Manzi
Poet

Aníbal Troilo
"Pichuco"
Musician and Composer

Julio Sosa
Singer

Carlos Gardel
Singer

Osvaldo Fresedo
Composer

El Polaco
Goyeneche
Singer

Astor Piazzolla
Musician and
Composer

Clothing

After some time, the tango also introduced a traditional attire: a wide-brimmed hat, a cut in the skirt, and a particular kind of shoe indispensable for Tango partners.

Feather

Head band

Little Scarf

Hairdo with chignon

Tuft and Gel Hairdo

Thin and straight moustache

White scarf with a monogram

Skirt with side cut. Comfortable and sexy.

Trousers loose at the top and tight at the bottom, allow us to see the movements of the feet.

High heel shoes, that fit tightly.

"Funyi" Hat

Jar of fixing gel for the hair

Comfortable kidskin shoes

El tango

These drawings show some of the relevant steps of the most famous dance in Buenos Aires. The style shown here is the Ballroom Tango of the twenties. It's an intimate dance of controlled eroticism far from the spectacular acrobatics, jumps, and contortions done basically in the Tango for export.

Double swinging sit: The man's right foot moves back till it reaches the same level of his left foot and meets the woman's left foot.

The Sit: The man's left foot makes a slight curve and the woman's right foot moves back forming a large curve.

The Exit: The man moves forward with his left foot and the woman moves back with her right foot.

The Double Step: The right leg crosses behind the left leg, it follows the direction of the arrow till the second "1" and moves back till the final position of the arrow at the third "1".

Circular swing: The man's right foot crosses behind his left foot and at the same time the woman's left foot moves backwards, then both turn.

"It is not a matter of being friends while dancing. The secret lies in a silence's sheath that makes us taciturn, almost resentful".
Juan Carlos Lamadrid.

A Media Luz (San Telmo)
Chile 316
Tel.: 4331-6146/1872

Armenonville (Recoleta)
Alvear 1879
Tel.: 4804-1033/4033

Bar Sur (San Telmo)
Estados Unidos 299
Tel.: 4362-6086

Casa Blanca (San Telmo)
Balcarce 668
Tel.: 4331-4621/4343-5002

Claroscuro (San Telmo)
Balcarce 971
Tel.: 4300-2816/8918

El Querandí (Monserrat)
Perú 302 esq. Moreno
Tel.: 4345-0331/1770

El Viejo Almacén (San Telmo)
Independencia y Balcarce
Tel.: 4307-7388

La Cumparsita (San Telmo)
Chile 302 esq. Balcarce
Tel.: 4361-6880

La Ventana (Monserrat)
Balcarce 425
Tel.: 4331-0217

Michelángelo (Monserrat)
Balcarce 433
Tel.: 4328-2646

Sabor a Tango (Barracas)
Av. Belgrano 2378
Tel.: 4942-2591

Señor Tango (Balvanera)
Vieytes 1655
Tel.: 4303-0231/34

Tangoteca (Puerto Madero)
Alicia Moreau de Justo 1728
Tel.: 4311-1988

Centro Cultural Torcuato Tasso
Defensa 1575 (San Telmo)
Tel.: 4307-6506

Noches de 2 x 4
Nights of 2 x 4
bailes - shows

Esquina Carlos Gardel (Abasto)
Carlos Gardel 3200
Tel.: 4867-6363

Esquina Homero Manzi (Boedo)
Av. San Juan 360
Tel.: 4857-8488

Café Bar Bajo San Telmo
(San Telmo)
San Lorenzo 365
Tel.: 4362-0537

Buenos Aires Sur
(Barracas)
Villarino 2359
Tel.: 4301-6758

Café Homero (Palermo)
Cabrera 4946
Tel.: 4773-1979

Caminito Tango Show (La Boca)
Del Valle Iberlucea 1151
Tel.: 4301-1520

Club del Vino (Palermo)
Cabrera 4737 - Tel.: 4833-0050

Club Villa Modelo (Villa Urquiza)
Arismendi 2684 esq. Avalos

El Chino (Pompeya)
Beazley 3566 - Tel.: 4911-0215

Kafetín (San Cristóbal)
Av. Independencia 2200
Tel.: 4308-2055

Clases de tango
Tango lessons

Círculo Bailable de la Armada
(Caballito)
José María Moreno 355
Tel.: 4903-6531

Club Almagro (Almagro)
Medrano 522
Tel.: 4774-7454

Confitería La Ideal (San Nicolás)
Suipacha 384 1°
Tel.: 4605-8234

La Galería (Caballito)
Boedo 722
Tel.: 4957-1829

Nuevo Salón La Argentina (Balvanera)
Bartolomé Mitre 1759

Acordes de Tango (San Telmo)
Humberto 1° 873
Tel.: 4307-5474

Centro Cultural Gral. San Martín
(San Nicolás)
Sarmiento 1551 piso 2, sala 14

La Escuela de Tango (Monserrat)
San José 364 3°
Tel.: 4383-0466

Morocco (Balvanera)
Corrientes 2048
Tel.: 4954-6911/2

Spell Café (Puerto Madero)
Alicia Moreau de Justo 740
Tel.: 4334-0512

Escuela Argentina de Tango
Centro Cultural Borges
Viamonte y San Martín
Tel.: 4312-4990

Zapatos rojos (San Telmo)
(milonga, shows)
Balcarce 460.
Tel.: 4372-6179

Club Gricel (San Cristobal)
La Rioja 1180
Tel.: 4857-7157

Souvenirs de tango
Tango souvenirs
(posters/ afiches)

Club del Tango (San Nicolás)
Paraná 123 5° of. 114
Tel.: 4372-7251

Galería Solar de French (San Telmo)

María de San Telmo
Pasaje de la Defensa (San Telmo)

El quiosco del Tango (San Nicolás)
Corrientes 1512 esq. Paraná

Centro de Exposiciones Caminito
(La Boca)
Lamadrid 784/90 esq. Caminito

Galería Caminito (La Boca)
Del Valle Iberlucea 1151
Tel.: 4301-1520

Chamote (San Telmo)
Defensa 861

Láminas antiguas (San Telmo)
Defensa 832

Buenos Aires Souvenirs (San Telmo)
Defensa 1066 local 10

Caminito Tango (La Boca)
Magallanes 827

Pasaje Obelisco Norte (San Nicolás)
Ella y yo, Local 5 y 7

Almacén de Tangos Generales
(San Telmo)
Plaza Dorrego

Tradiciones Argentinas
Ayacucho 1958 y Posadas 1167

Instituciones de tango

Academia Porteña del Lunfardo
Estados Unidos 1379
Tel.: 4383-2393

Academia Nacional del Tango
Av. De Mayo 833 1° piso
Tel.: 4345-6967

Casa Museo de Carlos Gardel
Jean Jaures 763

Tumba de Carlos Gardel
Av. Guzman 780 (Chacarita)

Argentine Folklore

Ritms and dances

Apart from the Tango, the Plata River folklore, you may find dances and music in Buenos Aires from every region of Argentina. Many are the rhythms. On the coast, the chamamé stands out, in the pampas, the zamba, towards the north, the chacarera, and at the border with Bolivia, the carnavalito. There are over hundred dances and native songs. Here, we only show a few that we consider to be representative.

Carnavalito

Pericón

Zamba

Malambo

Chamamé

Bailecito

Gato

Instruments and folk attires

Modern Creole Garments

Tubular Bass drum

Creole guitar

Charango" Front and back

Modern attires from the North

Quena

Siku

"Caja", two ways of playing it.

Old Creole attire

Flat Bass Drum

Bovine races and their cuts

Argentine meat is famous everywhere because of its outstanding quality. The natural breeding of livestock in the wide pastures of the pampas combined with a mild weather result in a meat, that makes it impossible for someone not to try an Asado Criollo (Creole Barbecue). For this purpose, there are a lot of good restaurants, grill rooms, and BBQ restaurants (see p. 140).

Holando Argentina

Polled Shorthorn

Red Polled

Aberdeen Angus

Charolais

Shorthorn

Santa Brigida

Hereford

Angus

Meat cut

Bife ancho

Azotillo

Nalga de adentro

Nalga

Lomo

Tira de asado

Peceto

Cuadril

Vacío

Bife angosto

Bola de lomo

Colita

The grill, achuras and inlays

Chorizos

Salchichas

Provoleta

Chinchulines

Tripa gorda

Morcillas

Matambre

Mollejas

Riñoncitos

The gaucho

Garments and mount

Although the archetypal character of the city is the tanguero, milonguero, or compadrito; in neighborhoods like Mataderos or in many folk parties (see page 134) you are bound to make contact with the archetypal character of the pampas: the Gaucho, with his original attire and all the equestrian culture he develops.

El apero

- Sudadera
- Mandiles
- Carona de cuero
- Cincha
- Hijar
- Lomillo
- Cojinillo

Girth

Cap made out of donkey's belly skin

Vest

Blouse or shirt

Belt

Waistband

"Chiripá" or Gaucho's pants

Colt boots

Knives and "Facones"

"Verijero" Knife

"Facón Caronero"

Stirrups

Stirrups made out of a ram's horn for two toes

Spurs

"Boleadoras" (Hunting slings)

Whips

"Rastra" for

Mate

What we call mate is an infusion with a nice taste and drinking it with friends has becoma such a widespread tradition that we might say it is a national custom. The Guaraní tribes discovered the plant it is made up of, which is called yerba, and they also found that its leaves are good for people's health.

The Jesuits later started to drink it as tea (in mate bags) and they created a system for growing the herb or plant (yerba paraguensi) that we use to make mate. The way we make and drink this infusion is also taken from the Guaraní tribes, which proves how ingenious their culture used to be. The gourd (also called mate), the straw (which we use to zip the drink), the kettle and the yerba are the basic elements you need if you want to drink some good mate.

Mateas a word has two different meanings: on the one hand, it is the drink itself and, on the other hand, it is the gourd, which also has different names according to the size, namely: the big ones are called porongos and those that have flat sides are called galletas.

Even though all mates were made out of pumpkins at the beginning, nowadays almost any material is good enough to pour some yerba and water in it. Some of them have silver decorations and others are entirely made up of silver or China.

The straw or bombilla is the means by which we zip the liquid. It has been a metal straw since the Jesuits' times, but the Guaraní tribes used to have cane straws. Sharing your mate and bombilla is a token of good manners, fraternity and peace.

Mate as a drink may take several names according to the way you make it, namely:

Bitter mate or cimarrón: just plain hot water and yerba.
Sweet mate: hot water, yerba, and sugar (white or brown).
Tereré: cold mate. You may use either cold water or citric fruits' juice.
Milk mate: hot milk and yerba.
Mate with coffee: yerba and hot coffee.
Mate Cocido: served as tea either in teabags or boiling the yerba. You may add some milk.

LA BOCA

Caminito Tango Show
Del Valle Iberlucea 1151
Te. 4301-1520/30
Cocina internacional /
International cuisine

Campo e Mare
Lamadrid 701 Tel. 4302-0785
Parrilla / Argentine barbecue

Cantina Gennarino
Necochea 1210 Tel. 4301-6617
Cocina Italiana / Seafood

El Obrero
Cafarena 64 Tel. 4362-9912
Cocina Argentina / Argentine cuisine

El Puentecito
Luján 2101 Tel. 4301-1794
Parrila / Argentine cuisine

La Barbería
Av. Pedro de Mendoza 19598
Tel. 4301-8870
Pescados y mariscos / Seafood

Il Matterello
Martín Rodríguez 517 tel. 4307-0529
Cocina italiana / Italian cuisine

Il Piccolo Vapore
Necochea 1190 Tel. 4301-4455
Cocina Italiana / Italian Cusine

La Ribera
Av. Pedro de Mendoza 1875
Tel. 4301-5160

La Cancha
Brandsen 697 Tel. 4362-2975
Pescados y Mariscos / Seafood

Valle de Palos
Aristóbulo del Valle 600
Tel. 4300-0671
Cocina Casera / Home made cuisine

Viejo Puente de Mario
Av. Alte. Brown 1499 Tel. 4301-2170
Pescados y mariscos / Seafodd

SAN TELMO • MONTSERRAT.

Asociación Sueca
Tacuarí 147 Tel. 4334-7813/9552
Cocina Sueca / Swedish Cuisine

Ban/Juu
México 1424 Tel. 4381-1259
Cocina Japonesa / Japanese cusine

Bidou de las Luces
Perú 269 Tel. 4801- 1844
Cocina Argentina / Argentine cuisine

Basque Francés
Moreno 1370
Tel. 4382-0244 / 383-5021
Cocina Vasco francés/ Basque cuisine

Campo dei Fiori
San José 491 Tel. 4381-1800/8402
Cocina italiana / Italian cuisine

Centro Asturiano
Solís 475 Tel. 4381-1342
Cocina española / Spanish cuisine

Club español
Bernardo de Irigoyen 180
Tel.:4342-4380

Vasco Fermín
Moreno 1370

Laurak Bat (Cocina vasca)
Av. Belgrano 1144
Tel.: 4381-0682

Como en casa
H. Yrigoyen 1315 Tel. 4383-2865
Cocina Argentina / Argentine cuisine

El acuerdo
Moreno 360 Tel. 4331-4172

El Caserío
H. yrigoyen 575 tel. 4331-1336

El Globo
H. Yrigoyen 1199 Tel. 381-3926
Cocina española / Spanish cuisine

El Querandí
Perú 302 Tel. 4345-0331/ 1770
Cocina Argentina / Argentine cuisine

El Rocío
Salta 151 tel. 4381-7502
Cocina Internacional /
International cuisine

La María
México 1310 tel. 4383-0173
Pastas

La Posada de Don Quijote
Lima 387 Tel. 4383-8602
Cocina internacional /
International cuisine

La Tasca
H. Yrigoyen 1218 tel. 4381-1290

Mesón Español
H. Yrigoyen 1211 1° tel. 4384-6667
Cocina Española / Spanish cuisine

Morocco
H. Yrigoyen 851 Tel. 4342-6046
Cocina exótica / Exotic cuisine

New Shushina
Solís 275 Tel. 4372-1056
Cocina Japonesa / Japanese cuisine

Plaza Mayor
Venezuela 1399 tel. 4383-0788
Cocina Española /
Spanish cuisine

Prosciutto
Venezuela 1212
Tel. 4383-8058
Cocina Italiana / italian cuisine

Rivero al Sur
Luis Saenz peña Esq. Estados Unidos
Cena Show / Dinner show

Status Virrey Ceballos 178
Tel. 4372- 6282 / 382-8531

Vieja Victoria
H. Yrigoyen 778
Tel. 4372-6282 /4316
Parrila / Argentine barbecue

PALERMO • LAS CAÑITAS

El Mistyco
(Cocina Porteña)
Gorriti 5902
Tel.: 4775-3653

Tango Republic (Mediterranea)
Julian Alvarez 1998
Tel.: 4864-4507

El Federal (Cocina criolla)
Honduras 5254
Tel.: 4382-6500

Almacén Cabrera
Cabrera 4399 Tel. 4832-4670
Cocina Criolla / Native cuisine

Al Shark
Av. Scalabrini Ortiz 1550
Tel. 4833-2049/6933
Cocina Arabe / Arabian cuisine

Azafrán
Honduras 5143 Tel. 4832-6487
Cocina casera / Home made cuisine

Bella Italia
Rep. Arabe Siria 3285
Tel. 4802-4253
Cocina Italiana / Italian cuisine

Buenos Aires News
Paseo de la Infanta
Av. Del Libertador y Av. De la Infanta
Tel. 4778-1500 / 0127
Cocina Internacional /
internationale cuisine

Cala
Soler 4065 Tel.4823-0413
Cocina Francesa / french cuisine

Campo Alto
Arenales 3360 Tel. 4821-6030 /6059
Cocina Argentina / Argentine cuisine

Cangas de Narcea
Av. Godoy Cruz 3108
Tel. 4773-4601 / 6706
Cocina Internacional /
International cuisine

Casona María María
Güemez 3140 Tel. 4821-3817
Cocina italiana / Italian cuisine

Centro de la Olla
Jorge Luis Borges 1559
Pizza y Pasta

Cielito Lindo
El Salvador 4999 Tel. 4832-8054
Cocina Mexicana / mexican cuisine

Club del Golf
Av. Tornquist 6385
Tel. 4775-0148 / 0197
Cocina Internacional / International cuisine

Cosa Nostra
Cabrera 4270 tel. 4862-1906
Cocina Italiana / italian cuisine

Cristophe
Fitz Roy 1994 Tel. 4771-1155
Cocina Francesa / French cuisine

Del Tomate
Salguero 2963 Tel. 4804-7882
Pastas

Dimitri. Puente Mitre
Av. Caseros y vías del ferrocarril
Tel. 4806-0022
Cena Show / dinner show

Dolli .Av. Figueroa Alcorta 3004
Tel. 4806-3366 / 3257
Cocina Internacional /
International cuisine

Domani
Salguero 3000 Tel. 4807-5288
Pizza y pasta

Don Battaglia
Av. Scalabrini Ortiz 803
Tel. 4773-0484 / 0597
Cocina Argentina / Argentine cuisine

Doney
Av. Del Libertador 3096
Tel. 4802-0075
Minutas / Fast Food

El Beduino
Av. Scalabrini Ortiz 1453
Tel. 4831-6951
Cocina Internacional /
International cuisine

El Lugar de Angel
Av. Del Libertador 4534
Tel. 4771-3179
Cocina Internacional /
Internatiional cuisine

El Oso del Charlie
Av. Del Libertador 4534
Tel. 4771-9184
Cocina Internacional /
International cuisine

El Sheik
Rep. Arabe Siria 3330
Tel. 4806-1398
Cocina Arabe / Arabian cuisine

El Taller
Honduras 4988 Tel. 4831-5501
Minutas / Fast food

Beckett bar, restaurant,
galeria de arte.
El Salvador 4960. Tel. 4831-7373

El Trapiche
Paraguay 5099 Tel. 4772-7343
Cocina Internacional /
International cuisine

Gascón
Av. Córdoba y Gascón
Tel. 4862-9662
Cocina Internacional /
International cuisine

Gitana Bs. As. News
Paseo de la Infanta
Av. Del Libertador Tel. 4778-1500
Cocina Española / Spanish cuisine

Guido's
Rep. De la India 2843
Tel. 4802-2391
Pastas

Where to eat

Habano
Seguí 4674 Tel. 4777-l043
Cocina Internacional /
International cuisine

Hermann
Av. Santa Fe 3902
Tel. 4382-1929
Cocina Alemana /
German cuisine

Incontro
Guatemala 5602 tel. 4775-7016
Cocina Italiana / Italian cuisine

Lusef
Malabia 1378 Tel. 4773-0450
Cocina Siria / Ssyrian cuisine

Jade
Ugarteche 3033 tel. 4803-2838
Cocina china / Chinese cuisine

Kalaat Yandal
Malabia 1467
Tel. 4831-1587
Cocina Arabe / Arabian cuisine

Katmandú
Av. Córdoba 3447
Tel. 4963-1122 / 3250
Cocina Huindú / Hindu cuisine

Kisher's
Av Cordoba 4660 tel. 4773-1888
Cocina Judía / Jewish cuisine

La Boguedita
Gascón 1460 Tel. 4867-1619
Cocina Cubana / Cuban cuisine

La Canzonetta
Av. Dorrego 1556 Tel. 4771-3998
Cocina Italiana / Italian cuisine

La Capillita
Av. Dorrego 2898 Tel. 4778-0068
Pescados y Mariscos / Seafood

La Casa Polaca
Jorge Luis Borges 2076
Tel. 4774-7621
Cocina Polaca / Polish cuisine

La Copa de Oro de Carlitos
Olleros 1667 Tel. 4772-5244
Parrilla / Argentine barbecue

La Furchina
Paraguay 3839 tel. 4776-2835
Cocina Italiana / Italian cuisine

La Mamá Rosa
Jufré 202 tel. 4773-2913
Cocina Argentina / Argentine cuisine

La Placita
Jorge Luis Borges 1636
Tel. 4832-6444
Cocina Italiana / Italian cuisine

Las Violetas
Av. Scalabrini Ortiz 2680
Tel. 4832-3968 / 1392
Parrilla / Argentine barbecue

La Tranquera
Av. Figueroa Alcorta 6464
Tel. 4784-6119
Parrilla / Argentine barbecue

Lindo Jardín
Cabello 3419 Tel. 4802-6851
Cocina China / Chinese cuisine

Morizono
Paraguay 3521 Tel. 4823-4250
Cocina Japonesa / Japanese cuisine

Museo Renault
Av. Figueroa Alcorta 3301
Tel. 4802-9629
Cocina Japonesa / Japanese cuisine

Nacachi
Jorge Luis Borges 1627
Tel. 4833-3311
Minutas / Fast food

Octavio
Salguero 2743 Tel. 4806-0035
Pastas
Oviedo
Beruti 2602
Tel. 4822-5415 / 4821- 3711
Cocina Española / Spanish cuisine

Paper Moon
Cerviño 3732
Tel. 4805-4643
Cocina Francesa / french cuisine

Park Zoo
Av. Sarmiento 2725
Tel. 4806-1835
Internacional cocina / International
cuisine

Pimienta
Paraguay 3512
Tel. 4824-7590
Cocina Argentina / Argentine cuisine

Pizza Cero
Cerviño 3701 Tel. 4803-3449
Pizzas

Pizza Donna
Av. Santa Fe 3202 Tel. 4822-4206
Pizzas

Plaka
Arévalo 2725 Tel. 4777-6051
Cocina Griega / Grek cuisine

Puerto Sol
Bulnes 2593 tel. 4802-8640
Cocina Argentina / Argentine cuisine

Provoletto
Huergo 190 tel. 4778- 3001
Parrilla / Argentine barbecue

Rincón Orgánico
Gurruchaga y Castillo
Tel. 4777-5082
Cocina Australiana

Rock Garden (Cocina Internacional)
Ugarteche 3154 tel. 4806-9178

Romario (Pizzas)
Cabello 3700 Tel. 4802-4732

Sahara
Cabrera 4223
Cocina Arabe / Arabian cuisine

Salguero y el Río
Av. Rafael Obligado y Salguero
Tel. 4801-5422 Minutas / Fast Food

Sarkis
Thames 1101
Tel. 4772-4911
Cocina Arabe / Arabian cuisine

Scuzi I
Cabello 3601 Tel. 4804-2900
Cocina Internacional /
International cuisine

Sítara
La Pampa 735 tel. 4784-2160
Cocina Hindú-Pakistaní /
Hindu-Pakistanese cuisine
Súbito
Salguero 2741 tel. 4806-0033
Pizza y Pasta

Tabaré
Charcas 3387 Telefax 4821-7598
Parrilla / Argentine barbecue

Tago Mago
Av. Rafael Obligado y Salguero
Tel. 4804-2444
Cocina Argentina / Argentine cuisine

Te Mataré Ramirez
Paraguay 4062
Tel. 4831-9156
Cocina Exótica / Exotic cuisine

The Horse
Av. Del Libertador 3880
Tel. 4773-4847
Cocina Internacional /
International cuisine

Xalapa
El Salvador 4800 Tel. 4833-6102
Cocina Mexicana / Mexican cuisine

Yamani
Julián Alvarez 1939 Tel. 4862-2848
Cocina vegetariana /
Vegetarian cuisine

Yasmin
Cabrera 4625 tel. 4832-5278
Cocina Libanesa / Lebanese cuisine

PUERTO MADERO
Agua Dulce
Av. Ing. Huergo 400 Tel. 4345-0900
Cocina internacional /
International cuisine

Bahía Madero (Pizzas)
Av. A. Moreau de Justo 292
Tel. 4319-8733

Bice
Av. A Moreau de Justo 192
Tel. 4315-6216
Cocina Italiana / Italian Cuisine

Divino Buenos Aires
Cecilia Grierson 28
tel. 4312-1221
Cocina internacional

Dizzy Lizzy
Av. A Moreau de Justo 846
Cocina Estadounidense /
American cuisine

Dock Café
Av. A Moreau de Justo 350/40
Tel. 4319-8719
Minutas / Fast Food

El Mirasol del Puerto
Av. A Moreu de Justo 202
Tel. 4315-6277
Cocina Argentina

Fechoría
Av. A Moreu de Justo 1140
Tel. 4342-8609/4949
Cocina Italiana / Italian cuisine

Hereford (Parrilla)
Av. A Moreau de Justo 1140
Tel. 4319-8715

Il Gatto Trattorías
Av. A Moreau de Justo 1192
Tel. 4345-6565/4949
Cocina Italiana / Italian cuisine

La Caballeriaza
Av. A Moreau de Justo 580
Tel. 4314-2648/50

La Casona de Roque
Av. A Moreau de Justo 256
Tel. 4315-6343
Cocine Italiana / Italian cuisine

La Parolaccia
Av. A Moreau de Justo 1052
Tel. 4343-1679/4742/1345
Cocina Brasilera / Brazilian cuisine

La Rosada
Av. A Moreau de Justo 1170
Tel. 4313-7200
Cocina Internacional /
International cuisine

Liberpool Pub
Av. A Moreau de Justo 350
Tel. 4319-8723
Minutas / Fast food

Piperno
Av. A Moreau de Justo 1942
Tel. 4313-0600

Puerto Cristal
Av. A Moreau de Justo 1080
Tel. 4331-3309/3669
Pizza y Pasta

Puerto Sorrento
Av. A Moreau de Justo 410
Tel. 4319-8730
Cocina Internacional /
International cuisine

Rodizio
Av. A Moreau de Justo 840
Tel. 4334-3646/3638
Cocina Internacional /
International cuisine

Spell Café
Av. A Moreau de Justo 740
Tel. 4334-0512
Cocina Internacional /
International cuisine

Spettus Steak House
Av. A Moreau de Justo 876
Tel. 4334-4210/4126
Cocina Brasilera /
Brazilian cuisine

Tocorro (Cocina Cubana)
Av. A Moreau de Justo 1050
Tel. 4342-6032

Where to eat

Xcaret
Av. A Moreau de Justo 164
Tel. 4315-6260/61
Cocina Internacional /
International cuisine

RECOLETA

A la Maracosa
M.T. de Alvear 225
Cocina Italiana / Italian cuisine

A'Mamma Liberata
J.E.Uriburu 1755
Tel.4804-3638
Cocina Italiana / Italian cuisine

Armenoville
Av. Alvear 1879
Tel. 4804-1033
Cena Show / Dinner Show

Au Bec Fin
Vicente Lopéz 1827
Tel. 44801-6894
Cocina Francesa / French cuisine

Babieca
Av. Santa Fe 1898 Tel. 4813-4914
Pizzas

Bonifacio
Guido 1939 Tel. 4805-2336 / 3996
Cocina Arabe / Arabian cuisine

Burger King
Av. Santa Fe 1997 Tel. 4812-5891
Fast Food

Campos del Pilar.
Buenos Aires Design
Av. Pueyrredón 2501
Tel. 4806-1111 int. 1276
Parrilla / Argentine barbecue

Caruso. Buenos Aires Design
Av. Pueyrredón 2501
Tel. 4806-3299
Cocina Italiana / Italian cuisine

Champs Ellysees.
Buenos Aires Design
Av. Pueyrredón 2501 Tel. 4806-1111
Minutas / Fast food

Clark's Recoleta
Junín 1777 Tel. 4801-9502
Cocina Internacional /
International cuisine

Como
Juncal 2019 Tel. 4806-9664 / 7954
Cocina Internacional /
International cuisine

El Beso
Pacheco de Melo 2909
Cocina Exótica / Exotic cuisine

El Bodegón de Peña
Peña 2475 Tel. 4806-7536
Cocina Argentina /
Argentine cuisine

El Living
M. T. de Alvear 1540
Tel. 4811-4730

El Tranvía
Av. Santa Fe 2933 Tel. 4823-6347
Pizza y Pasta

Fellini
Paraná 1209 Tel. 4811-2222
Cocina Italiana / Italian cuisine

Hard Rock Café.
Buenos Aires Design
Av. Pueyrredón 2501
Tel. 4807-7625
Cocina Estadounidense /
American cuisine

Harper's Junín
Junín 1773 Tel. 4801-7140
Cocina Internacional /
International cuisine

Hippopotamus
Junín 1787 Tel. 4801-1040
Cocina Internacional /
International cuisine

La Barra
Av. Del Libertador 932
Tel. 4812-1745
Cocina Española /
Spanish cuisine

La Biela
Av. Quintana 596
Tel. 4804-0449
Minutas / Fast food

La Mansión. Park Hyatt Hotel
Cerrito 1455 Tel. 4326-3610
Cocina Francesa / French cuisine

La Parolaccia
Riobamba 1046 Tel. 4812-1053
Cocina Italiana / Italian cuisine

Lola
R. M. Ortíz 1805 tel. 4804-3410
Cocina Internacional /
International cuisine

Luckie's. Buenos Aires Desin
Av. Pueyrredón 2501 Tel. 4806-1111
Cocina Estadounidense /
American cuisine

Mc Donald's
Av. Córdoba 2031 Tel. 4964-0625
Fast Food

Mora X
Vicente Lópéz 2152
Tel. 4803-0261 / 2646
Cocina Francesa / french cuisine

Munich del Pilar.
Buenos Aires Design
Av. Pueyrredón 2501
Tel. 4806-1111 / 6910

Open Plaza
Av. Del Libertador 1800
Tel. 4802-7501 / 03
Fast food

Pizza Banana
Ayacucho 1425 Tel. 4812-6321
Pízza y Pasta

Porto Bello
J. E. Uriburu 1629 Tel. 4806-4275

Rodizio
Av. Callao 1292 Tel. 4814-1776
Cocina Internacional /
International cuisine

Romanaccio
Av. Callao 1021 Tel. 4811-9888
Pizza y Pasta

Sahara Continental
Junín 1733 Tel. 4801-7544
Cocina Internacional /
International cuisine

Sensu
Posadas 1101 Tel. 4815-5161
Cocina Japonesa / Japanese cuisine

Teatriz
Riobamba 1220 Tel. 4811-1915
Cocina Internacional /
International cuisine

The Kilkenny. Irish Pub
M. T. De Alvear 399 Tel. 4312-7291
Restaurante Irlandés y Continental

The Shamrock
Rodríguez Peña 1220 Tel. 4812-3584
Cocina Irlandesa / Irish cuisine

Tiro Loco
Vicente Lópéz y Azcuénaga
Cocina Mexicana / Mexican cuisine

Troyka
Juncal 1647 Tel. 4414-1009
Cocina Rusa / Russian cuisine

RETIRO • PLAZA SAN MARTIN

A Mi Manera
Av. Del Libertador 308
Cocina Italiana / Italian cuisine

Blue Oyster
M. T. De Alvear 399
Tel. 4312-9179
Pescados y Mariscos

Club del Retiro
Juncal 743 Tel. 4326-7869
Parrilla / Argentine Barbecue

Dixie Diner
Av. Del Libertador y C. Pellegrini
Tel. 4322-3646
Cocina Estadounidense /
American cuisine

Don Corleone Blues Bar
Reconquista 924 Tel. 4311-8802
Cocina Italiana / Italian cuisine

Druid Inn
Reconquista 1040
Tel. 4312-9844
Cocina Internacional /
International cuisine

El Aljibe- Sheraton Hotel
San Martín 1225
Tel. 4318-9000
Cocina Internacional /
International cuisine

Filo (Pizzas)
San Martín 975
Tel. 4311-0312 / 1871

Frontera
Esmeralda 941
Tel. 4313-0013
Cocina Internacional /
International cuisine

Galani. Marriot Plaza Hotel
Posadas 1086 Tel. 4326-1234
Cocina Italiana / Italian cuisine

Jan Toki
Posadas 1029 Tel. 4393-0332
Cocina Vasca / Basque cuicine

La Brasserie. Marriot Plaza Hotel
Florida 1005 Tel. 4318-3000
Cocina Internacional /
International cuisine

La Chacra
Av. Córdoba 941
Tel. 4322-1419 / 2593
Parrilla / Argentine barbecue

La Payanca
Suipacha 1015 Tel. 4312-5209
Cocina Criolla / Native cuisine

La Querencia
Esmeralda 1392
Tel. 4393-3205 / 3202
Cocina Criolla / Native cuisine

La Terraza Anush.
Lancaster Hotel
Av. Córdoba 405 Tel. 4311-3021
Cocina Argentina-Arabe /
Argentine-Arabian cuisine

Las Nazarenas
Reconquista 1132 Tel. 4312-5559
Cocina Argentina /
Argentine cuisine

Ligure
Juncal 855 Tel. 4393-0644
Cocina Internacional /
International cuisine

Morizono
Paraguay y Reconquista
Tel. 4314-0924 / 4443
Cocina Japonesa / Japanese cuisine

Orleans.
Aspen Towers Hotel
Paraguay 857
Tel. 4312-9172

Piola
Libertad 1078
Tel. 4812-0690
Cocina Italiana / Italian cuisine

Plaza Mayor
Posadas 1052 Tel. 4393-5671
Cocina Española /
Spanish cuisine

Romario
Montevideo 1655
Tel. 4814-5210
Pizzas

Sensu
San Martín 760
Tel. 4319-5103
Cocina Japonesa
Japanese cuisine

The Tower Lounge.
Sheraton Hotel
Av. Leandro N. Alem 1193
Tel. 4318-9000 int. 2510
Cocina Internacional /
International cuisine

MUSEUMS

Museo de Arte Moderno
Museum of Modern Arts
Av. San Juan 350
Tel.: 4361-1121

Museo Histórico Nacional
National Historic Museum
Defensa 1600
Tel.: 4307-1182

Museo Penitenciario "Antonio Ballve"
Penitenciary Museum
"Antonio Ballve"
Humberto 1° 378
Tel.: 4362-0099

Museo de Arte Hispanoamericano
"Isaac Fernández Blanco"
Museum of Spanish-American Art
"Isaac Fernández Blanco"
Suipacha 1422
Tel.: 4327-0228/0272

Museo Participativo de Ciencias
Participative Museum of Science
Junín 1930
Tel.: 4807-3260/4806-3456

Museo Nacional de Bellas Artes
National Fine Arts Museum
Av. Del Libertador 1473
Tel.: 4803-0802/8814

Museo Nacional de Arte Decorativo
National Decorative Arts Museum
Av. Del Libertador 1902
Tel.: 4806-8306/4801-8248

Museo de Arte Oriental
Oriental Arts Museum
Av. Del Libertador 1902 Piso 1°
Tel.: 4801-5988

Museo de Motivos Argentinos
"José Hernández"
Museum of Argentine Heritage
"José Hernández"
Av. Del Libertador 2373
Tel.: 4802-7294/4803-2384

MALBA, Museo de arte
latinoamericano de Buenos Aires.
Av. Figueroa Alcorta 3415 (Palermo)
Tel.: 4808-6500

Museo de Artes Plásticas
"Eduardo Sívori"
Museum of Plastic Arts
"Eduardo Sívori"
Av. De la Infanta Isabel 555
Tel.: 4774-9452

Museo Casa de Yrurtia
Yrurtia´s House Museum
O´ Higgins 2390
Tel.: 4781-0385

Museo de Arte Español
"Enrique Larreta"
Spanish Art Museum
"Enrique Larreta"
Juramento 2291
Tel.: 4783-2640/4748-4040

Museo Histórico Sarmiento
Sarmiento Historic Museum
Juramento 2180
Tel.: 4783-7555

Museo Histórico de la Ciudad
de Bs. As. "Brigadier Gral.
Cornelio de Saavedra"
Crisólogo Larralde 6309
Tel.: 4572-0746

Museo de Ciencias Naturales
"Bernardino Rivadavia"
Museum of Natural Science
Angel Gallardo 470
Tel.: 4982-1154

Museo Xul Solar. Laprida 1212
Tel.: 4824-3302

ART GALLERIES

Del Infinito: Av. Quintana 325
Dabbah Torrejon: Bustamante 1187
Principium: Esmeralda 1357
Gara: Pje. Soria 5020
Belleza y felicidad: A.de Figueroa 900
Elsi del Río: Arevalo 1748
Braga Menendez Schuster: Darwin 1154
Atica: Libertad 1240
MAMAN Av. del Libertador 2475
De Santi: M.T.de Alvear 868
El Socorro: Suipacha 1331
Gal.Museo Aguilar: Suipacha 1178
Klemm: M.T. de Alvear 636
Lagard: Suipacha 1216
Le Point: Suipacha 1250
Leonardo Avalos: Arroyo 858
Palatina: Arroyo 821
Praxis Arte Internacional:
Arenales 1311
Rubbers: Suipacha 1175
Ruth Benzacar: Florida 1000
Artistas Plásticos: Viamonte 458
Suipacha: Suipacha 1248
Van Eyck: Sta.Fe 834
Van Riel: Talcahuano 1257
Vermeer Galería de Arte:
Suipacha 1168
VyP: Arroyo 971
Zurbarán: Cerrito 1522
Espacio Giesso: Defensa 1326
Sara García Uriburu: Uruguay 1223
Art House: Uruguay 1223

CINEMAS

Alto Palermo: Av. Santa Fe 3235 -
827-8362
Ambasador: Lavalle 777 - 322-9700
América: Callao 1057 - 811-3818
Atlas Belgrano: Av. Cabildo 2165 -
781-7200
Atlas Lavalle: Lavalle 869 - 322-1936
Atlas Recoleta: Guido 1952 -
803-3313
Atlas Santa Fe: Av. Santa Fe 2015 -
823-7878
Auditorio Maxi: Carlos Pellegrini
657 - 326-1822
Belgrano Multiplex: Obligado y
Mendoza: 781-8183
Capitol: Av. Santa Fe 1848 -
812-2379
Cineplex: Lavalle 727 - 393-8610
Complejo Tita Merello: Suipacha
442 - 322-1195
Electric Lavalle: Lavalle 836 -
322-1846
Galerías Pacífico: Florida 735 - 319-
5357
Gamount: Rivadavia 1635 - 371-
3050
General Paz: Av. Cabildo 2702 -
781-1412
Grand Splendid: Av. Santa Fe 1860 -

812-0808
Leopoldo Lugones: Av. Corrientes
1530 - 374-8611
Lorange: Av. Corrientes 1372 -
373-2411
Lorca: Av. Corrientes 1428 -
371-5017
Los Angeles: Av. Corrients 177/70 -
371-3742
Losuar: Av. Corrientes 1743 -
4371-6100
Maxi 1-2-3: C.Pellegrini 657 -
4326-1822
Metro: Cerrito 570 - 4382-4219
Monumental: Lavalle 780 -
4393-8865
Normandie: Lavalle 855 -
4322-1000
Ocean: Lavalle 739 - 4322-1515
Paseo Alcorta: Av. F. Alcorta y
Salguero: 4806-5665
Patio Bullrich: Av. Libertador 750 -
4815-8328
Premier: Av. Corrientes 1565 -
4374-2113
Santa Fe: Av. Santa Fe 1947 -
4812-8980
Savoy: Av. Cabildo 2829 -
4781-9400
Solar de la Abadía: Luis M. Campos
y Maure - 778-5181
Trocadero: Lavalle 820 - 4393-8321.

THEATERS

Astral: Av. Corrientes 1639 -
4374-5707
Ateneo: Paraguay 918 - 4328-2888
Avenida: Av. de Mayo 1222 -
4381-0662
Blanca Podestá: Av. Corrientes 1283
4382-2592
Broadway: Av. Corrientes 1155 -
4382-2345
Cátulo Castillo: Bmé. Mitre 970 -
4345-2774
Cervantes: Libertad 815 - 816-4224
Colón: Libertad 621 - 382-5414
Del Centro: Sarmiento 1249 -
417-7097
Del Globo: M.T. de Alvear 1155 -
4816-3307
Del Pueblo: Diag. Norte 943 -
4326-3606
Del Sur: Venezuela 1286 -
4383-5702
El Excéntrico: Lerma 47
Empire: H.I Yrigoyen 1934 -
4953-8254
General San Martín: Av. Corrientes
1530 - 4371-0118
Gran Rex: Corrientes 900 -
4322-8000
La Plaza: Av. Corrientes 1660 -
4371-7623
La Trastienda: Balcarce 460 -
4342-7650
Liberarte: Av. Corrientes 1555 -
4375-2341
Liceo: Rivadavia y Paraná -
4381-4291
Lola Membrives: Av. Corrientes
1280 - 383-2025
Maipo: Esmeralda 433 - 322-4882
Manzana de las Luces: Perú 294 -
342-9930
Margarita Xirgu : Chacabuco 875 -
300-2448
Metropolitan: Av. Corrientes 1343 -
371-0816

Off Corrientes: Av. Corrientes 1632
- 4373-3608
Opera: Corrientes 900 - 4326-1335
Payró: San Martín 766 - 4312-5922
Picadilly Teatro: Av. Corrientes 1254
- 4373-1900
Piccolo Teatro: Av. Corrientes 1624 -
4373-3465
Presidente Alvear: Av. Corrientes
1659 - 374-6076
Megafón: Chacabuco 1072.

SHOPPINGS / MALLS

Abasto
Av. Corrientes 3247
Tel.: 4959-3400

Alto Avellaneda
Guemes 897
Avellaneda

Alto Palermo
Arenales 3360
Tel.: 4821-6030/6059

Buenos Aires Design Recoleta
Av. Pueyrredón 2501

Caballito Shopping Center
Av. Rivadavia 5108

Galerías Pacífico
Florida y Av. Córdoba

Paseo Alcorta
Jerónimo Salguero 3172

Easy Home Center
Av. Bullrich 345 y Cerviño
Paseo La Plaza
Av. Corrientes 1660

Patio Bullrich
Av. Del Libertador 750 y
Posadas 1245

Solar de la Abadía
Luis María Campos y Maure

Spinetto Shopping Center
Moreno 2301
Tel.: 4954-3252 al 59

PASEOS - SIGHTS

Jardín Zoológico
(Garden Zoo)
Av. Las Heras y Av. Sarmiento
Tel.: 4806-7412

Jardín Botánico
(Botanic Garden)
Av. Santa Fe 3951
Tel.: 4832-1552

Jardín Japonés
(Japanesse Garden)
Av. Casares y Av. Adolfo Berro
Tel.: 4804-4922/9141

Paseo del Rosedal
The Roses Garden
Parque Tres de Febrero-
Av. Del Libertador y
Paseo de la infanta

Planetario "Galileo Galilei"
"Galileo Galilei" Observatory
Av. Sarmiento y Roldán
Tel.: 4771-6629/4772-9265

Tridimensional Guide of Buenos Aires

Reserva Ecológica
Ecological Reserve
Av. Tristán Achával Rodríguez 1550
Tel.: 4315-1320

Feria Paseo del Retiro. Mercado de
pulgas y artesanías.
Antártida Argentina y Av. de los
Inmigrantes. Fines de semana

Feria de mataderos. Artesanía y tradiciones populares.
Av. de los Corrales y Lisandro de la
Torre. sábados, domingos y Feriados.

Feria de la Baulera. Hogar de la
Misericordia. Azcuénaga 1654.
Antigüedades y usados, Sábados y
domingos desde las 11 hs.

Mercado de pulgas de Dorrego.
Niceto Vega y Dorrego.
Todos los días

HOTELES ★★★★★
Alvear Palace H.: Av. Alvear 1891 -
4804-4031
Caesar Park Buenos Aires -
Posadas 1232 - 4814-5150
H. Etoile:
Pte. R.M. Ortiz 1835 - 4804.-8603
Sofitel: Arroyo 845 - 4804-1600
Claridge: Tucumán 535 - 4314-7700
Libertador Kemplinsky Buenos Aires:
Av. Córdoba y Maipú -4 322-2095
H. Panamericano:
C. Pellegrini - 4393-6017

Marriot Plaza:
Florida 1005 -
4318-3000
Park Hyatt Buenos Aires:
Posadas 1088 - 4326-1234
Sheraton Buenos Aires & Towers:
San Martín 1225 -
4311-6311.
Hotel Intercontinental:
Moreno 809 - 4340-7100
Hilton:
Juana Manso y Macacha Güemes.

HOTELES ★★★★
Ap H. Las Naciones: Av. Corrientes
818 - 4325-2491
Ap H. Benco: H.Yrigoyen 1534 -
4476-1192
Ap H. Arenales: Arenales
4855 - 4322-7196
Ap H Bauen Suite: Av. Corrientes
1856 - 4804-1600
Ap H. Esmeralda: M.T. de Alvear
842 - 4311-7632
Ap H. Obelisco Center:
Pte. Roque S. Peña 991 - 4382-9100
Ap H. Plaza San Martín:
Suipacha 1092 - 4312-4767
Ap H. Recoleta: Guido 1948 -
4803-2397
Ap H. Suipacha: Suipacha 1235 -
4393-3088
Ap Ulises Recoleta: Ayacucho 2016 -
4803-4457
Bisonte: Paraguay 1207 - 4394-8041
Bisonte Palace: M.T. de Alvear 902 -
4311-4751
Carlton: Libertad 1180 - 4812-0081

Gran Hotel Buenos Aires: Alvear 797
- 4312-3003
Gran Hotel Colón: Carlos Pellegrini
507 -4 325-1017
Gran Hotel King: Lavalle 560 .
4393-4012
Bristol: Cerrito 286 - 4382-5401
Carsson: Viamonte 650 -4322-3551
Castelar: Av. de Mayo 1152 -
4383-5000
Hotel Continental: Av. R.S.Saenz
725 - 4326-3250
Crillon: Av. Santa Fe 796 -
4312-8181
De las Américas: Libertad 1020 -
4393-3432
Hotel Dorá: Maipú 963 -
4312-7391
Hotel El Conquistador:
Suipacha 948 - 4328-3012
La Fayette:
Reconquista 546 -
4393-9081
Lancaster: Córdoba 405 - 4311-3021
Nogaró: Diag. J.A. Roca 562 .-
4331-0991
Posta Carretas: Esmeralda 726 -
4394-1625
Presidente: Cerrito 846 -4 372-5081
Recoleta Plaza:
Posadas 1557 - 4804-3471
Regidor: Tucumán 451 - 4314-7917
República: Cerrito 370 - 4382-4011
Rochester:
Esmeralda 542 -
4326-6076
Salles: Cerrito 208 - 4382-0091
Savoy: Callao 181 - 4372-7788

HOTELES ★★★
Benco: H. Yrigoyen 1534 -
4476-1192
Camino Real: Maipú 572 -
City: Bolivar 160 - 4383-6481
Embajador: C. Pellegrini 1181 -
4393-9485
Gran Argentino: C. Pellegrini 37 -
4345-3073
Gran Eibar: Florida 328 - 4325-1698
Orly: Paraguay 474 - 4312.4344
San Carlos: Suipacha 39 - 4345-1022
Ap. Embassy: Av. Córdoba 860 -
4322-1228
Columbia Palace: Corrientes 1533 -
4373.-2123
Concord: 25 de Mayo 630 - 4313-
2018
Constitución Palace: Lima 1696 -
4305-9011
Hotel Deauville: Talcahuano 1253-
4812-1560
Eleven Palace: La Rioja 87 - 4864-
5097
Esmeralda Palace: Esmeralda 52 -
4393-1085
Impala: Libertad 1215 - 4812-5696
Italia Romanelli: Reconquista 647 -
4312-6361
Liberty: Corrientes 632 - 4325-0261
Monumental: Junín 357 -
4 953-8472
Napoleón: Rivadavia 1364 -
4383-2031
Normandie: R. Peña 320 -
4374-7001
Plaza Francia: Pje. Schiaffino 2189 -
4804-9631

Gay Friendly

Amerik: disco - gay mixto
Tel: 4865-4416
Dir: Gascón 1040

Angels: disco - gay hombres
Dir: Viamonte 2168

Bach Bar: pre dancing - gay mixto
Tel: 155877-0919
Dir: Cabrera 4390 (Palermo)

Casa Brando: gay mixto
Tel: 4858-0610
Dir: Luis María Drago 236
(Almagro)

Cero consecuencia: pub - gay mixto
Dir: Cabrera 3769 (Palermo)

Coco: bar resto - gay mixto
Tel: 4331-1071
Dir: Rivadavia 878

Contramano: disco-gay hombres
Dir: Rodríguez Peña 1082 (Recoleta)

Deep Blue: bar, juegos -gay mixto
Tel: 4827-4915
Dir: Ayacucho 1240

Eternity: fever night - gay mixto
Tel: 4832-0320
Dir: Bartolomé Mitre 3514

Glam Dance: disco - gay hombres
Dir: Cabrera 3046

Gasoil New Generation: Bar
Tel: 4864-4056
Dir: Bulnes 1250 (Barrio Norte)

Kim Novak: Bar - gay mixto
Tel: 4773-7521
Güemes 4900 (Palermo)

L`averno: bar_resto - gay mixto
(show: lucha en el barro)
Tel: 4371-1278
Dir: Av. Corrientes 1632

Marlene: gay mujeres (club lésbico
argentino)
Tel: 4932-2219
Dir: Colombres 770

Oxen: disco - gay
Tel: 4382-2233
Dir: Sarmiento 1662 (Tribunales)

Punto G: pub - gay mixto
Tel: 4829-2240
Dir: Anchorena 1347 (Barrio Norte)

Palacio Buenos Aires: disco-gay
Tel: 4334-0099
Dir: Adolfo Alsina 934 (Monserrat)